MANAGING
Incompetence

An Innovative Approach for Dealing With People

Gabriel Ginebra

PRESS

ASTD Press is an internationally renowned source of insightful and practical information on workplace learning, performance, and professional development.

ASTD Press
1640 King Street Box 1443
Alexandria, VA 22313-1443 USA

Ordering information: Books published by ASTD Press can be purchased by visiting ASTD's website at store.astd.org or by calling 800.628.2783 or 703.683.8100.

Library of Congress Control Number: 2012953505

ISBN-10: 1-56286-869-1
ISBN-13: 978-1-56286-869-7
e-ISBN: 978-1-60728-749-0

ASTD Press Editorial Staff:
Director: Glenn Saltzman
Manager, ASTD Press: Ashley McDonald
Community of Practice Manager, Human Capital: Anthony Quintero
Associate Editor: Stephanie Castellano
Editorial Assistant: Sarah Cough
Text and Cover Design: Lon Levy

Printed by Versa Press, Inc., East Peoria, IL, www.versapress.com.

Contents

Foreword

I met Gabriel Ginebra in the early 1980's. We were students together in Northern Spain, and engaged in long conversations about our intellectual pursuits. Our professional lives drove us in different directions and we did not meet again until three decades later. By then, both of us had traveled tens of thousands of miles around the world. Since reuniting, we have kept our friendship going, mostly via email and, when circumstances allow, at restaurants in Barcelona or Madrid, the cities where we each reside.

I feel privileged to write the foreword for one of Gabriel's works. I am a great admirer of both his work and his qualities as a person; among them, the permanent hope to submit ideas and methods that are not always politically correct. Especially in a time like this, when a great number of people in high government offices appear to be worthy of the title contributed by Gabriel, some readers will find this examination of incompetence unnerving. His fondness for heterodoxy has long been his trademark, at least since I have known him.

As you devour these pages, you will see that Gabriel's writing method involves threading anecdotes and other personal experiences around a core of academically-supported theories. This structure brings the concepts in this book to life.

The author urges us to look long and hard into a mirror before we judge others mercilessly. Hopefully, Gabriel's contribution will help us kick the perverse habit of labeling, usually in the worst way possible, our colleagues, managers, and subordinates.

In the text, it is emphasized that managing people is a science with an artistic edge. He who considers management either an art or a science can never govern well. Truly effective management combines academic knowledge, method, and consistency with creativity, intuition, and spontaneity. After all, there is such a thing as human nature, but there is no such thing as a human machine. Individuals must be treated as such.

The rebellious mood in the text will be pleasing to many and, hopefully, displeasing to none. Gabriel does not beat around the bush. His often blunt language may affront those not truly willing to improve their management and professional skills. However, his honest account of his past mistakes and lessons learned from them will disarm many readers. Gabriel's language is not acrimonious; but it is irreverent enough to engage readers and honest enough to awaken their self-awareness.

The unpretentious language of this work makes it accessible to all. You do not need be an expert in managing people and organizations to understand this book. It can be of interest to anyone involved in an organization. Even those who have nothing to do with organizations may also find the lessons in the following pages valuable, for they contain guidelines and techniques that can be applied to all kinds of interactions, not only those within the workplace.

In the following pages, the reader will find many motivations for facing the exciting challenge of understanding a person in his or her complexity, thereby avoiding the mistake of conceptualizing the human being as a simple entity. Whoever makes and acts on that assumption always ends up hurting mankind, to say nothing of wreaking havoc in one's immediate work environment.

In this cocktail shaker of a book, you will find quotes and assessments from the field of religion, which is uncommon in this type of text. I expect you will find that most of these citations are relevant to the content and insightful.

For my part, I can only wholeheartedly congratulate the author, wishing that he will very soon delight us again with his thoughts. Gabriel is an outstanding representative of a group of authors within the yet-to-be structured movement known as the "Spanish School of Management." Almost all of its leading members, as I am positive Gabriel will also soon be, belong to exclusive professional organizations, such as the Top Ten Business Experts (www.toptenbusinessexperts.com).

Gabriel's book is much more than a self-help book. Its friendly tone and accessible format, not to mention the valuable and actionable information within its covers, will revolutionize your management style and help you create a rewarding work environment for your employees.

Javier Fernández Aguado, Managing Partner of MindValue

Introduction

In Praise of Incompetence

We have a warped concept of managers. We imagine them young, handsome and slim, wearing impeccable suits and speaking rapidly into smartphones at an airport terminal. They have a university degree and an MBA. They know about marketing and finance, and regularly present at high-powered meetings. They are extremely competent.

Now let us look at those we work with every day in the office, the flesh and blood managers we've had, and at ourselves. Are they similar to the image described, or did we miss it by a long shot?

Let us also consider the entrepreneurs whose names and faces we know. Do we imagine them with a Colgate smile, exuding confidence, wealth, and power, driving an expensive sports car, and owning the latest technologies? Or do they look like more down-to-earth people: disheveled, simple, low profile, with receding hairlines and visible discomfort wearing a tie?

We have such a gilded idea of business executives that we would not be able to recognize them on a bus or in the supermarket line. It is difficult to imagine them just walking around some town. Yet they are, and this book is for and about them. This book presents a more realistic boss type: someone who is not always brimming with business acumen; someone with doubts, who tries and sometimes fails; who harbors a private conviction of his ongoing personal shortcomings; and who is always putting out fires. In other words, someone who is incompetent.

It may seem like the blind leading the blind, as people manage-ment is fundamentally incompetence management. Shallowness, for-getfulness, hurriedness, and lack of common sense surround us, along with people's good qualities. We have to deal with incompetence not only because it is abundant, but because competence requires less ef-fort to manage.

This book is tremendously optimistic. It argues that we can do bet-ter, and that best is the enemy of good. Its tone is critical, but not defeat-ist. As Irving Caesar says, "The optimist believes we live in the best of all possible worlds; the pessimist fears it to be true." A story from Franco's Spain tells of an industry minister who went directly to the head of the government—Francisco Franco himself—and asked for investments to improve the RENFE (the Spanish national railway system). Franco looked at him condescendingly and replied, "Dear Minister, RENFE cannot be improved."

We are all incompetent because we can all improve, and because we are always learning. We do not want the word "incompetence" to be pejorative. In this book, we define a "competent" person as an incompetent person who is insufficiently diagnosed; an "incompetent" person is someone with high potential who is insufficiently worked. We're not as good as we think, but we can be better than we think.

Finding one's self among the kingdom of incompetent people will bring peace to the readers of this manuscript. You will also gain hope to undertake the process of self-improvement and assume responsibility for improving those around you. You must work with what you have.

Managing People as a Science

In business, we operate with a total lack of rigor when analyzing its most important asset: people. Here, anything goes and everyone thinks they know everything. Good attitude and communication are considered the "magic bullet" to resolve any difficulties that may arise.

But there is no such cure-all. People in the workplace have a plethora of ills: lack of focus, lack of resources, too little training, disengagement, and so forth. People are especially weak collaborators. Just this morning I was analyzing a promotional problem with a group of executives, in which no one criticized anyone present and everyone agreed, despite defending positions as diverse as keeping the worker on the job, to demoting or firing him.

Despite such chaos, there is a science to managing people (though not an exact science). There is a systematic approach we can take when addressing incompetence. And as the science of medicine shows us, without a proper diagnosis in hand we can't issue the appropriate treatment. So, this book focuses first on getting to the root of various forms of incompetence.

What Will You Find in This Book?

The structure of the contents is simple and organic, and organized into three distinct parts:

    I.   Recognizing Incompetence in Yourself and Others

    II. Diagnosing Incompetence: The Fougi Template

    III. Tools to Manage Incompetence

Part I: Recognizing Incompetence in Yourself and Others

Recognizing our own incompetence is the beginning of all wisdom. My experience shows how difficult it is to recognize our own faults. We have in our minds a long list of what our colleagues do wrong, but we don't dare create the same list for ourselves.

The first chapter builds our self-awareness of how we manage others, and what we do wrong, especially if we suffer from the syndrome of being surrounded by incompetent people.

The next chapter examines how the paradigm of management relegates actually managing people to the background. It details how mainstream corporate training is disorienting because, among other things, it relies too much on economic theories.

The third chapter invites us to get closer, with renewed interest, to the people who surround us: spending time with them, listening to them during face-to-face conversations, and discovering the talent locked inside those who may be considered talentless.

Part II: Diagnosing Incompetence: The Fougi Template

Any scientific approach starts with a good diagnosis. There are many different kinds of incompetence. In this central part of the book, 10 short chapters are strung together to present a gallery of incompetent characters (the theoretical one, the suffocated one, the clumsy, the distracted, and so forth), along with their respective treatments.

Part III: Tools to Manage Incompetence

Everything is treatable in people management. The third part of this book discusses some people-management tools that should be revalued. One is the approach called "Teach Work First." Most so-called motivational and performance problems stem from not knowing *how* to work—in other words, from lack of training.

The two final chapters deal with emotional management leverage for the employee: saying "please," "thank you," "good job," apologizing, and forgiving. Toward the end, we advocate apologizing as a way to operate on an equal level of respect with employees.

The book ends with a surprising reformulation of managing talent.

How to Read the Book

It's much easier to explain how I wrote the book than to explain how to read it, because it has a life of its own beyond its author. Its core comes from materials created for skills development courses. It is therefore working material, focused on self-analysis and immediate application.

I've been surprised when I am told that the book can be read in one sitting: "I only stopped for dinner," someone confessed. Although it is a fast-read book, it is not at all a fast-cooked one. Its development has been long, written while I was relaxing, thinking, almost meditating. It is my best attempt to unearth core truths about people management. In my research I appealed to popular wisdom and classical thought, in which I have found more fresh ideas and innovative practices than in the countless texts on currently popular management topics.

This work presents a new management philosophy: one of patience, humility, rewarded generosity, and trust in those who are around. It is the philosophy of peaceful and wise leadership, to be slow to anger and quick to forgive. This is evidenced in those for whom managing is a profession and a vocation, rather than a step on the way to achieving something else.

Incompetence may be all around us, but mostly it is within us. The problem is always us. It must be assumed. No alibis. Change yourself and be one less problem in your business. Fortunately, having a disease does not prevent us from healing ourselves or others.

Now: Welcome to the club for incompetent people. Let's see if we can help each other.

Part I

Recognizing Incompetence in Yourself and Others

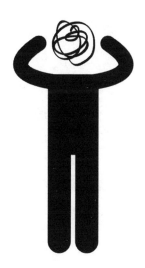

Work With What You Have

"The optimist believes we live in the best of all possible worlds; the pessimist fears it to be true."

(Irving Caesar)

You probably picked up this book because you think you are surrounded by incompetent people. It's true. But you must know something from the start—this is the twofold approach of this book—in this story, you are the most incompetent of them all.

But there's no need to worry too much about it, because everybody is to some degree incompetent. It is said—and it is also one of the principles in this book—that you must work with what you have. This idea is extremely practical so long as you include yourself in this category of mediocrity.

The great deeds of mankind were not accomplished by a handful of geniuses, but by a bunch of incompetent people. Albeit, incompetent people with a bit of luck, a bit of coordination, and a bit of management.

In this book we will see why child prodigies end up being total disasters, and how someone who is both blind and deaf ends up in a position of respect and power. There are ordinary people who do extraordinary things, and others who think themselves extraordinary and yet are truly average. The difference has much to do with how they are managed.

All managers want to manage their staff well, but we must admit that very few do. Declaring that we want people to be the primary asset has become common, but with no real follow-up in most cases. We say, but we do not do.

Good Intentions Are Not Enough

Goodwill does not result in good management. If we do not learn to manage people, we will be haunted by continual conflicts that we lack the skill to solve. I've seen good-natured directors hated by their employees, and others not empathetic at all who have a huge emotional-towing capacity.

> "Goodism" and voluntarism are two major
> obstacles in managing employees well.

This book is aimed at managers of people. I want to help you walk the path to both desiring and achieving the objective; to help you in the process of turning your good intentions into effective management habits.

> There is an art and a science to managing employees well.

In these pages I intend to show that managing people requires a specific and rigorous professional approach. Aggressively attempting to fix the flaws of your employees can backfire, but "anything goes" is also not the attitude with which to manage. There are rules to management people well. They are neither many nor complicated, but they are difficult to apply because they call into question our management methods and, even more, how we are as people. Following the steps in this book does not guarantee success in managing people, but not following them guarantees failure.

It is essential to follow the principles of science; however, learning is not consummated until it is converted through practice into a personal art. I want to be very specific and avoid the big concepts and new paradigms of leadership that promise to solve all our problems in one sweep. Specificity is needed because managing people well is not an abstract challenge. It is a very concrete endeavor requiring the patience of an entomologist or, better yet, that of a mother with her children. The typical intellectual, theoretical approach is not suitable here.

The content in this book is based on what might be called the science of managing people, and can be summed up in such basic and immediate actions as:

- dedicating more time to people
- knowing your subordinates individually and personally
- diagnosing their flaws
- teaching them to work
- knowing how to reward, punish, and appreciate.

Georges Chevrot wrote a lovely book that I have enjoyed for years titled *Small Virtues of the Home*. This book could also be called *Small Virtues of Managing People*. This place of coexistence, the home— including the family home and what we might call the "work home"—is built on small virtues. Most marriages, which are relationship projects between two people, fail due to small details. There are usually no initial ideological differences to predict subsequent success or failure. When a break occurs, we seek explanations at the beginning of the relationship, as if there were a sign that should have forewarned a bad outcome. The answer is not there. It's usually in the little things, and their accumulation over time.

Any significant relationship is woven with a lot of connective tissue. People get together for big reasons but fall apart due to small ones: inattention, small resentments, lack of gratitude, misunderstandings. And the same goes for every failed boss-employee relationship.

Managing Genius Is in the Details

As the poet Miquel Martí i Pol said, "Perhaps the only mystery is that there is no mystery." The solutions we present in this book are not grand, sweeping, earth-shattering, or transformative. They can be implemented simply and quietly during everyday workplace interactions. And they work in the same way: simply, quietly, rewarding you in small ways over time, if you are patient and diligent. No amount of genius can replace the attention to detail.

In the spirit of small-great remedies, we offer five small-large proposals that will change how you, the reader, deal with people management. It would suffice to incorporate two of them into your managing repertoire. If you can already see clearly what they may be, you are allowed to skip the rest of the book.

Five Laser Tips to Improve People Management

1. Dedicate one afternoon per week to be with your staff.
2. Next month, take those who depend on you out to dinner, one by one.
3. For each one of your employees, create a file of their shortcomings so that you can work on resolving them.
4. Accept that an employee does something important better than you, and admit it in public.

5. Dedicate time to teaching a particular skill to an employee whom you had targeted for not mastering it, and complete this task within an appropriate time frame.

Manage Incompetence Because Competence Manages Itself

We talk about managing incompetence as synonymous with managing people, but there is incompetence on both ends of the employer-manager relationship. The person who manages is also an incompetent person, like a plumber who learns by trial and error and in the process ruins your bathroom.

Speaking about incompetence is more interesting, more realistic, and more practical; it means talking about ourselves and the flesh-and-blood people before us; it means disabusing ourselves of the notion that somewhere out there is someone who is wholly competent. These people exist only in textbooks.

> **Only when we begin to understand our own inadequacies and those of others, will we learn to manage the people who depend on us.**

At the start of a typical leadership course, participants are asked to think about good leaders they have known throughout their careers. In my case, this exercise doesn't work. I don't know about your experience, but I've only had two types of leaders: bad and really bad, at least if measured with the standards used in these courses. One way or another, we are all incompetent—even high-potential and high-performing employees.

Echoing Socrates, we could say that the beginning of all learning is the recognition of one's ignorance. Denying incompetence is denying the very possibility of learning. You can't ask for things to go well from the start; you have to err and try again. You should be able to claim the right to incompetence and the right to make mistakes, although some people may find that strange.

Do We Have Competent Managers?

If you need more proof that incompetence rages in the everyday workplace, take a look at these statistics, from a study conducted by the consulting firm TMI:

- Two out of 10 people want to leave their current company.
- Six out of 10 say negative things about the company outside its walls.
- Nine out of 10 don't feel responsible for their organization.
- Only one in 10 is proud to work at his company.

Disturbing, is it not? If the above figures apply to your company—and why wouldn't they—you clearly have your work cut out. Like in the famous novel *And Then There Were None,* by Agatha Christie, we don't know who among us are seeking other jobs or speaking badly about the company. But they're the majority. If you have a group of 10 workers, statistically you will have six who are dissatisfied in some way and two who are thinking about leaving. It would be dangerous to consider yourself the exception to the rule—especially as buying this book is a sign that you suspect you are the majority.

	Employee %	Number of Employees	Who Might They Be?
Want to leave the company	20%		
Speak badly about the company	60%		
Don't feel responsible for the company	90%		
Are proud of the company	10%		

Don't you think it's important to immediately examine and improve your people-management skills? If you want, you can wait for another survey, but you're guaranteed to get the same results.

Reality is stranger than fiction. In a seminar, a participant approached me to say he had no problem employees. He was a manager of more than a hundred people. According to him, all were highly motivated, so he saw no need to watch over them or meet them personally. I found this a clear cause for alarm, like the person who doesn't go to the doctor because he is afraid of being diagnosed. When a risk is serious—and this one definitely was—being over-cautious is better than being neglectful.

Another study, by Otto Walter, found that 40 percent of employees can't stand their bosses, and 30 percent believe that they work under the direction of an incompetent person. In the Cisneros report, published in the newspaper *El País* on January 12, 2008, 36 percent of workers said they would send their manager to a psychiatrist. There is a close relationship between employees who want to leave the company and those who grade their bosses poorly. Their desire to leave the company stems from their dislike of their supervisors. There are numerous of surveys that show management style is the main reason for dropouts. According to Nuria Chinchilla, a professor at IESE in Barcelona, 30 percent of voluntary turnover is due to this cause. Other studies reached similar conclusions.

> **We don't leave a business; we run away from a boss.**

A boss can make or break employee satisfaction and performance. For a while now we've been seeing evidence of deteriorating employee-manager relationships: employees fail to report to work without calling in, they refuse to take on challenging work, turnover rates are skyrocketing, and so on. Bosses can take much of the blame for this.

The "Being Surrounded by Incompetent People" Syndrome

There is often as much dissatisfaction of managers with their employees as there is of employees with their managers. Perhaps you've experienced the feeling that no one around you can do anything right. The feeling strikes during particular scenarios: when you've returned after an absence to find that your instructions have been carried out wrongly, or you summon an IT professional to solve a technical problem, only to have the solution last two days. Or you realize that an idea you were communicating in an email has evaporated during a subsequent round of emails. Or you find your team is making the very mistakes you repeatedly warned them against. You feel that the second you drop the ball, things will be done incorrectly or not at all.

> **A manager who believes that half his staff
> is incompetent, is surely incompetent himself.**

He who complains of being in charge of a bunch of useless fools reveals personal inadequacy. It's like the parent who complains that his son is rude, when he is primarily responsible for that child's education.

Or like the saying, "You're all selfish; the only one here who thinks about me is me."

A study by Otto Walter conducted in 2007 showed that 90 percent of managers consider themselves to have "toxic" employees. If not downright toxic, many managers feel that their employees have become increasingly dense, and that the art of "work well done" has been lost. We wonder how our employees even arrived in our departments, and we wish they hadn't.

During my earlier career years, I trained bank managers with four or five employees each. Among other activities, we rated the competence of their employees. Some managers were harshly critical. Their proposals for addressing problems were to abort the problems: to get rid of the employees.

Throughout the program I met with all the managers in the area, so I proposed they implement a rotation system: create a metaphorical "bench" where each manager could leave undesirable employees, and another could take them. I suspected the less-than-favorable skills assessment depended heavily on the evaluators themselves, and that most of the managers had worse opinions of their employees than deserved. In many cases, we must turn our critical eye on ourselves, make do with the team we have, and stop coveting the neighbor's team.

To Change People or Exchange People? That Is the Question

To change people or to exchange people; that seems to be the dilemma of managing people. We propose that the best way to develop real talent is by moving forward and developing the people we already have. There are no shortcuts to realizing an employee's full potential.

Let's train our workforce; let's work with what we have.

The key to outperforming the competition is to get the average employee to perform better than the competition—to develop talent where there apparently is none. You have to discover the full potential in front of you, which you often fail to see. In other words, you have to work with what you have.

We often hear that people don't change; they do what they do, produce the same quality of work, and perform at the same rate. It's also said that people do what they can, and he who does what he can, can't do better. "You can't teach an old dog new tricks." Nothing is further from the truth! Skills and behaviors are perfectly malleable.

There is little evidence showing that behavior is fixed from the start. The reality is that people thought to be good, go bad, and bad people can become good; certain mediocre employees can sometimes achieve brilliant results, and even the most talented ones often fail. As a young man, I was told (and I did not believe it then) that in the long run, the most brilliant people often don't succeed; but the ones with average talent who defeat laziness, do. Talent is more a product of hard work than a magical quality that is gifted at birth. The success or failure of an employee is largely a result of the challenges and the people he meets along his career, not a result of his predetermined talents.

Soccer is a clear example of how potential does not always ripen into talent. Much of a player's ability depends on the strategies, attitudes, and above all, team dynamics and leadership that he experiences. There are hundreds of examples of athletes sharing the same talent who have had very different paths to success.

It's Hard to See Talent When It's So Close

Many managers suffer from hyperopia (farsightedness): They appreciate talent better when it's far away than when it's up close. They underestimate the qualities of people on their teams, while overestimating other managers, or employees of other companies. They long for those out of their reach, while those who are close get their flaws pointed out. It's the romantic trend of novelty, the naïve "out with the old, in with the new" approach.

"I love humanity, but people annoy me," could very well be the motto of many managers who fill their mouths with praise for "human capital," while failing to appreciate the professionals around them. We must learn to appreciate the employees who are in our care.

Furthermore, it's advantageous to believe in the talent of the talentless. Think of the Pygmalion effect: If you treat someone as if they have talent, they end up becoming someone with talent. Everybody is capable of revealing the talent they have inside.

In his book, *The Servant*, James Hunter writes, "Imagine treating Chucky on the forklift as if he was the president of the company, or our students like they were school board members, or nurses like they were doctors, or soldiers like they were generals." We must follow J.W. Goethe's advice: "Treat a man as he is and he will remain as he is. Treat a man as he can and should be, and he will become as he can and should be."

Those linear stories that tell of extremely competent people who ascend the ladder of professional success often seem to hide some level of falsehood. I'm more attracted to the losers who spend their life trying, who accumulate certain successes and many more failures; those who live for second chances, who started when they were too old, those who were rehired, the reinvented, and the averagely talented. I am attracted to stories like that of the Catalan Olympic medalist Mireia Belmonte's, who started swimming as a way to correct a back problem she was diagnosed with at an early age. Or Basque cyclist Leire Olaberriá, a bronze medalist in the Beijing Olympics who left a competitive athletic life behind at 26 due to medical problems and struggled to learn a new discipline, until becoming an Olympic champion at 30: "I'm back in cycling thanks to a little help from a lot of people who have pushed me to where I'm now" (*Gara*, 19-VIII-08).

> **Reality is stranger than fiction.** José Ángel Carrey, an attorney both blind and partially deaf, once said in an interview, "When I started my college education, a Roman law professor condescendingly said, 'Look, Carrey, you might pass a class, but you won't make it to the end.' I replied, 'Thank you, professor. We will see how far I make it.'" However, his parents believed in him: "Despite the fact that I was born premature at five and a half months, that I lost my sight in the incubator and meningitis left me somewhat deaf, they raised me with serenity and firmness." They'd had a baby and they would fight along his side until he became an adult. "I was very lucky to have them" (Interview with José Ángel Carrey, *La Vanguardia*, *La Contra*, 16-II-08).

Do you believe in the competence of those closest to you? What comes to mind when you think of the word talent?

- Do you think of a huge multinational organization, or your own business?
- Do you think of Germany, or Japan, or your own country?
- Do you think of graduates from a world-class business school, or graduates from the local community college?

The Unbearable Lightness of Managing People

Dilbert's boss calls him to a meeting to acknowledge that he was mistaken when he announced that his employees were his most valued asset. "In fact," he says, "you're the ninth." What's the eighth? "Carbon paper" (Adams, 1993).

Despite repeated statements that human resources are a company's most valuable asset, managing people is still a skill that is lacking in most managers. And it remains so because we barely understand it, and we are reluctant to do it. We have significant theoretical and practical reasons to avoid dedicating ourselves to others.

Why do we not dedicate ourselves to people?

- The predominant concept of the term *manager* downplays the importance of people skills.
- Companies don't usually require specific dedication to this task.
- Management training is misleading, statistics are overused, and the human factor is underestimated.
- Managing people is slow, cumbersome, and "uncool."

A Manager Who Marginalizes People

Managers see themselves as heads of budgets, salespeople, and structure developers, rather than as teachers, creators of working environments, or conflict mediators. They like to be seen as technology experts but find it harder to understand their role as people developers. They devote time regularly to reviewing catalogs, numbers, and facilities, but fail to visit with or talk to their employees. They might admit they're bad with people, but never that they're bad with sales or profits.

I suggest an exercise: See which of the stereotypes described below are closest to what comes (spontaneously) to mind when you think of a manager:

- a person having a chat in a garden, or two friends drinking beer in the afternoon
- someone sitting at a computer working on an Excel document, or someone giving a PowerPoint presentation in a meeting.

In today's culture, the images associated with managerial work typically involve:

- transportation elements such as an airplane or airport, taxi or large sedan
- technology devices, such as smartphones, tablets, and laptops
- PowerPoint presentations, charts, and process diagrams
- executives in expensive suits in a boardroom
- glass-walled office buildings and industrial plants.

Conduct an image search of the word "manager," or take note of how a manager is portrayed in a TV show or movie. They portray a serious, crisply-dressed person in a dark suit and tie, somewhat aloof, with an air of self-importance. The message transmitted about managerial work is that it's a complex job, centered on numbers, with a bunch of graphics and calculations, briefcases, and long written reports. A computer is ever-present. The technological aspect is highlighted, not only in the general ambiance but also in the products. Scenarios depict large, maybe multinational companies with a clear preference for sectors like IT, finance, and professional services. It makes it seem like a manager spends his hours behind a screen, writing reports and emails.

We already know that this image does not match reality. We're not looking at real managers, just actors. But these images, though inaccurate, do recreate reality. They make us value and expect certain unrealistic, and rather irrelevant, qualities in our managers.

The Manager's Self-Image

This biased view is not unique to script writers; it is deeply rooted in our minds. If we asked somebody to paint what comes to mind when he hears the word *company*, it's likely that he will draw a factory with smoke stacks, or computer screens, or stark glass buildings. Is it not peculiar that when we think about a manager, we imagine him poring over a report rather than speaking with another person?

These images convey a message about expected behaviors in the workplace, ideas about when a manager is doing his job and when he is not. If my self-image as a manager does not include having a beer with my employees, I would avoid that activity, especially during work hours. If reading in the middle of the afternoon is not listed in my imaginary job description, I would feel guilty if I did it and I would think of it as wrong for another person to do. If laughing with a group of co-workers in the hallway made others suspect that we were slacking on the job, I'd stay in my office.

To study the self-image that managers have of their work, I used a simple test, found on the next page, that compares concept pairs. Choose which one best corresponds to your vision of professional responsibility.

Task Aspect	People Aspect
Business acumen	Emotional intelligence
Hard skills	Soft skills
Communicate in business terms	Communicate in layman's terms
Hiring consultants	Consulting staff
Working independently	Working on a team
Good negotiator	Good listener
Reviewing numbers	Reviewing people
Budgeting	Making people provisions
Developing products	Developing people
Knowing the premises	Knowing certain people

The results are revealing. Task-based skills involve efficiency, accuracy, a razor-sharp focus on numbers; while people skills involve communicating clearly, understanding behaviors, coaching, and listening well. Popular culture portrays managers who demonstrate task-based skills.

Being a Good Leader Is Not Just About Being a Good People-Manager

We must put the people-management aspect of any type of managerial work into perspective, and distinguish it from equally essential management activities, such as budgeting, initiating and overseeing projects, and conducting technical work.

Work for many managers hardly consists of people-management activities, even if they tell themselves otherwise. Their time is divided between tasks like developing business strategies, maintaining public relations, and monitoring budgets. There often is not time left over for developing and motivating their subordinates. Many high-level executives do not have direct relationships with their employees.

Managers will always have to perform certain frontline functions unrelated to administrative or people-management activities. In industries such as banking, insurance, or real estate, managers are especially qualified salespeople. They are promoted based on their selling ability. Some managers are rather used to exercising their technical talent, and invest more time and effort in this than in managing their subordinates. For example, the director of the training company prefers providing the bulk of the training, and the consulting director performs as the star analyst.

There are essential management roles that have little to do with the art of leading people. The qualities of the sales director as a product expert or principal negotiator, for example, are different from the ones required to be a good people manager. To excel as a negotiator you do not have to be a good people manager; but to be a good people manager, you must know the technical side of your craft. A good manager must also be a go-getter, a resourceful person, one who always has a friend, an idea, an experience that comes in handy. Finally, he must be an entrepreneur; he must know the business well and earn profits. That does not imply he is a good people-manager. In fact, businessmen and entrepreneurs tend to be individualistic. They are so far ahead that everyone else gets left behind.

Many become managers because of their product and market knowledge. In many industries, management positions are won by those who demonstrate technical talent and prowess, not by those who exhibit excellent people skills. Behind many successful businesses, there is a product-knowledge ace. However, many businesses fail because of the same product-knowledge ace, who doesn't have the same knowledge of the people who work for him.

To our detriment, we often confuse great skill and talent with being a good leader. Toscanini, the great musician, was a genius but a bad manager. He was uncompromising and rude to his musicians, who only tolerated him because of his dazzling vision of music. He would express an idea for the sound and would attempt to force it out of his team. He tried to solve problems by yelling and beating his baton.

It is very easy to have Toscanini's bad attitude, but it is very difficult to match his talent. Leadership is often confused with knowing how to yell. But if you don't have the talent Toscanini had, it is wise to settle on a softer approach to leadership.

Nonetheless, leading a company takes more than getting along with people. As we've seen, there are many leadership roles that are just as important: salesperson, negotiator, coordinator, and strategist. If managers fail in these roles, any investment they make in their employees will be useless. Without technical skills and business acumen, managers will be unable to retain their employees.

Reality is always stranger than fiction. The CEO of a known financial management firm was well loved by his employees. He knew them all, visited their offices; they were his priority. But he had a highly risky business approach: all offices were company-owned, inviting third-party risk. He did not take into account the cyclical nature of the sector, and after spectacular growth in good times, he took a dip during the recession and ended up selling the company for one euro.

Engaging in People Management

Managing people is a specific activity. Many managers don't like it, and they barely get involved. Maybe not everyone has what it takes. As we saw in the anecdote above, placing too much focus on befriending employees can distract from the task of managing the business. Well-known managerial models demonstrate this, such as Robert Blake's and Jane Mouton's *Managerial Grid* (1964), or Paul Hersey's and Ken Blanchard's *Situational Leadership* (1977).

A sensible option may be to share functions. At the core of corporate empires we always find a product-expert manager plus another person who acts as the glue, being more people-centered. Sony, for example, had Masaru Ibuka, the genius inventor, while Akio Morita was the one dedicated to building an international organization. Microsoft had Bill Gates as the product expert, while Steve Ballmer mobilized people. Successful organizations always have someone at the top who is dedicated to managing people in very specific ways.

To help us close this section, an anecdote that dates back to medieval times underlines the effectiveness of separate executive roles.

During a conclave, the cardinals could not decide between three outstanding candidates: one for his saintliness, the second for his great culture, or the third for his practicality. The indecision ended when a cardinal stood up and said: "It is useless to keep hesitating; our case has already been referred to in the 24th letter of Bernard of Clairvaux. We just need to apply it, and everything will be as smooth as silk. Is the first candidate a saint? Well, then, *oret pro nobis* (let him pray for us); let him pray for our poor sinners. Is the second one a sage? Great, *doceat nos* (let him teach us); let him write a book on erudition. Is the third one prudent? *Iste regat nos*; let him govern us and be the Pope" (Luciani, 1978).

Abusing Math

"They Have Not Learned How to Lead" was the title journalist Jordi Goula picked to express the low opinion employees have of their managers (*La Vanguardia*, 30-XI-03). How and when do we learn to lead, and in particular, to lead people? In business school? At the office or at home? Through corporate training or independent reading?

Formal education has many gaps in this regard. Employees' daily issues, anger, fears, and ambitions are not listed in university courses and are used only as anecdotes in management schools. There is plenty of literature on how to train employees, how to tell them about their poor performance, or how to fire them. Yet many of these books fail to help with their naïve voluntarism and big concepts surrounding leadership, excellence, and competence.

Most business administration and management classes focus only on economics and mathematics. Instead of cultivating the soft skills crucial for effective leadership, students spend their time analyzing mathematized economic theory models.

One of the reasons it is difficult to develop people management skills in university classrooms is because participation is often not required. Discussion is just a voluntary complement, because the subject is understood as a sequence of facts to be received passively. How can students be expected to learn how to communicate if they never open their mouths during class?

Henry Mintzberg denounced the growing academization of business schools in his insightful work, *Managers Not MBAs*, a hard look at the soft practice of managing and the development of managers. He claims that the problem is the teaching paradigm, which is highly dependent on the economic model. The management concept taught in higher education is suffering from number-overload. It suggests that a company can be measured by numbers alone.

Let's recall that Harvard Business School was founded with the express intent of seceding from the School of Economics. In 1908, a small group of teachers left the School of Economics, convinced that the lessons taught therein were irrelevant to business. And across the river, they founded the embryo of what would become the most prestigious business school in the world. The case-study method they invented was gathered from experiences related by managers, who were invited to fill the initial content void.

We have to mention here the thoughts of Professor Antonio Valero, founder of IESE Business School at the University of Navarra in Barcelona. For him, the essence of business management is political science, even above production or accounting knowledge. In his view, political reasoning should dominate management studies: strategies, consensus, procedures, institutions, and so on. Math is but an instrument and should be used in good measure. As Valero would put it, "All the math you need to know in order to manage is adding, subtracting, multiplying, and dividing. And if you are very fast at multiplication," he would add ironically, "you can forget about division." Therefore, as director of IESE, he warned that if one day a teacher approached him with a derivative, he would be fired on the spot.

Even in 1916, Henri Fayol, the creative genius behind basic management concepts, reported the abuse of math as the main obstacle to training good leaders: "Nobody can deny that mathematics is one of the most important branches of education; it is the great instrument of progress for physical and mechanical sciences, and all who are devoted to industry need to have more or less broad notions on this subject. However, we must not lose sight of the meaning of measure. Philosophy, literature, natural history, and chemistry are also major factors of social progress; is this a pretext to impose on our future engineers many years of forced education on each of these subjects...? Mathematics is abused with the belief that the more you master this subject the more it is suitable for business management, and that its study develops and rectifies judgment to a greater degree than any other subject. These are errors that cause serious harm to our country, and I find it useful to fight them... A long personal experience has taught me that the use of higher mathematics is null in business management."

Managing People Is Hard

Managing people is uncomfortable. Dealing with numbers, data, or stocks is more comfortable and predictable; they do not get discouraged when you tell them they're obsolete. When you yell at a machine, it does not flinch. But if you become angry with an employee, he is hurt, perhaps irreparably so. Marketing plans and budgets are simply easier to deal with than humans.

In logistical problems, when you apply the same solution, you get the same result. But with a people problem, applying the same remedy does not guarantee you the same result.

People are complicated. Every individual has a unique personality, background, and life experience. Political correctness requires us to consider our employees as neither male nor female, neither young nor elderly, neither mothers of large families nor single parents. We are taught to keep our personal and professional lives separate. Yet if an employee is experiencing a serious personal problem, we would be wrong to expect him to perform as well as before.

Shapes, shades, nuances, moments, and contexts, *do* matter when managing people. The objective and the subjective do matter. Mechanical cause-and-effect relations do not rule. Juan Antonio Pérez López spoke about how analyzing an interaction with a cat from a physics point of view, as if the cat were simply a mass, would be a mistake. If we kick that mass, it may move in a direction opposite to that expected, attacking us or leaping upward. When dealing with living beings, the laws of physics do not always apply.

Managing people is also uncomfortable and frustrating because people do not change their behavior quickly. They take two steps forward and one step back. If we want to lead people well, we must comply with the following principles:

- Communicate frequently and honestly.
- Implement detailed, iterative plans.
- Allow for mistakes.
- Keep up the good humor.

Everyday demands do not make it easy for us to focus on people; we need to target this activity explicitly. There are reasons why people management is not always prioritized in organizations: the two largest are that it is not an explicit responsibility, and efforts to this end are not measured or rewarded. Managers may not discern any material gain from engaging their employees. Instead, managers focus on hitting numbers or production and quality targets. Those are the efforts that are tracked and rewarded; that is where their incentives lie.

Personnel Director or People Manager?

"I love humanity, but people annoy me."

(Charles M. Schulz)

For decades, human capital has been gaining priority in corporate speeches. We are used to hearing about motivation, leadership styles, and business philosophy. The first thing you find out about a company through its website is its vision and values. There are entire projects and departments devoted exclusively to organizational development, remuneration policies, and cultural management. However, these human resource systems, implemented to increase employee engagement and satisfaction, often miss their target. We implement sophisticated communication programs while still failing to listen; we invest in a complex assessment system, yet employees still feel their work is unappreciated; we audit training yet can never find the person with the right skills when we need him.

The proliferation of programs to develop human resources sometimes creates a false commitment to employees. Documents are filled out, meetings held, procedures followed, and policies created, yet they barely touch on the difficulties people undergo on a daily basis. New training is offered, which does not address daily inefficiencies: Joe's clutter, Jane's tardiness, or that other guy who is shy or doesn't know how to plan ahead.

Reality is stranger than fiction. In a project conducted by the world's largest consulting firm for a large financial institution, they were debating whether the level curve slope within the competition should be interpreted as a linear or quadratic function. Meanwhile, the talented development director fell victim to harassment from a co-worker, and shortly after leaving the organization, took it to court.

Programs quickly lose sight of their original intentions. They fail to fulfill their objectives and become just another chore to be performed in the spirit of compliance. I perform an evaluation on you, but I will not tell you what I really think of you. I attend the course, but I will not apply what I learn. I comply with the procedure but fail to meet the target. We obtain a certificate of quality; however, the actual quality has not changed. Objective programs are implemented that are overly formal and sophisticated, and are unrelated to our work and the goals we pursue every day. It takes a lot of effort to revise goals. Yet it is urgent to revisit them frequently, revitalize our people-management procedures, and perhaps liquidate those that have lost their relevance.

When I studied for my MBA, a friend declared that all people-management problems supposedly stem from issues with motivation or communication. He called it "MOCO"—an amalgam of the words *mo*tivation and *co*mmunication. But the fact is that motivation and communication are rarely the cause of such problems. Rather, their root causes tend to be very specific and concrete: lack of training, lack of experience, or lack of resources.

The extensive use of abstract terms and concepts used in the business world today prevent proper diagnosis of people-management problems, and hinder critical thinking. For example, in the business courses I teach, if a theoretical problem is considered to be due to lack of communication, I ask my students, "Who needs to communicate with whom? What will they communicate about, how, when, and where?" Usually they have trouble critically analyzing the scenario and coming up with the right answers.

On Being Specific

What is not specified is not performed. This is a catchphrase for one of my friends, Juan Antonio González Lobato, and it could well be this book's catchphrase. Because managing people requires being specific. Being specific on what you want done, how to begin it, when to finish it.

We are immersed in the big-business model, where people problems are met with statistics, programs, and strategies. But we should live by the small-business model, where people have faces and eyes, and they have a first and last name. Being big or small is not so much a question of size as one of mentality. Many small businesses are managed as if they were big, and some big ones lead their people as though they were small.

People can't be managed by concepts, reports, or procedures; they are managed by relationships. Good people management is a matter of specifics, of careful attention to detail; it requires listening, sympathizing, and making simple efforts to get to know one another. The impact of informal relationships on formal dynamics never ceases to amaze me. Meetings with someone with whom you've shared coffee and personal conversation often have a much better outcome than those with someone to whom you've hardly spoken. Companies, both large and small, will continue to manage their people poorly until they learn to reach out to them as if they were a small business. Only then will they integrate staff, have less turnover, and achieve success with less effort.

People's attitudes at work are formed by small virtues and lots of pettiness. Vanity ruins many achievements, and it's hard to empathize with a vain manager. On the positive side, we see that sympathy, though not included in the job description, motivates workers to help each other. Basically, we all seek friendliness at work, and our behavior changes directions if we are unable to find it.

Reality always outdoes fiction. Antonio is an exemplary employee at a law firm. He is a quiet, discreet, tireless worker. He never complains about anything. Recently, another employee of the same rank was promoted. And Antonio announces his intention to leave the company. At first, it seems that he's acting out of envy, yet he's not ambitious. During the exit interview, the human resources manager discovers the problem is that he needed a friend in management, someone he could trust. The issue was not the missed promotion, but that he was not considered. Management avoids making this explanation and labels Antonio as greedy.

Today it seems that a manager can run a hotel the same way he can run a dry-cleaning chain. Management is taught as if it were disconnected from reality, as if all companies were equal because they can all apply the same accounting and human-resource development principles. That is not the case. Managers are not as interchangeable as they would like to believe. Each business is very specific and only by knowing it by heart can you make it work well. As an example, Warren Buffet never invests in any business he doesn't fully understand. He never invests in technology because he's not familiar with it.

The definitions of skills, corporate culture, and values don't distinguish between companies and sectors. They all sound alike—and they all sound vague. How can we implement effective human capital programs with such vague guidelines? How can we define specific competencies for specific industries, professions, and roles?

Reality always outdoes fiction. Once on a plane, I had to sit behind some human resources executives in their 30s. They were heading to the annual meeting of their multinational company. During takeoff and landing, the flight attendant had to ask for their attention because they kept looking at the PowerPoint presentation they were to give the next day. They were analyzing its 20 core competences. There was nothing flashy: team-building, making things happen, interpersonal skills, and so forth. To those, they had to add other sector-specific things, plus some industry-specific and job-specific skills: over 40 in total. These were all phrased in the same style and seemed perfectly interchangeable. The executives spoke as if they were antique collectors: "Where did you find these skills? They're so cool!" The answer: "From a consulting firm manual and from a food company."

Corporate statements give no clue about the business in question. What type of business would match the 10 values below?

1. Customer Focus

2. Worker Support

3. Service Culture

4. Teamwork

5. Strict Adherence to Legality

6. Management by Example

7. Good Working Environment

8. Management by Objectives and Motivation by Results

9. Austerity and Prudence

10. Creativity and Simplicity

The values could apply to virtually any company. Can't we be more creative, more specific, and more efficient in creating values? Perhaps, a cosmetics company should strive for aesthetic taste; an audit firm, accuracy; and a knowledge-intensive company, the desire to know.

Perhaps because of generic values and goals, we find it difficult to find the right training to suit specific professional development needs.

Normally, a single course is offered on leadership for both service and industrial companies; the same content is distributed to large firms, small public businesses, family-owned companies, and employees in the audiovisual industry or the furniture industry. As the lone exception, I know of a master's degree in business management in the meat sector.

Who Is Responsible for Managing People?

We must rediscover the personal, nontransferable, and specific responsibility that every line manager has over his human resources. He is the one who knows the work process, the most common errors made, which employee needs to improve in which areas, and who is talented in which areas. He must be well-acquainted with their micro-skills, as well as their bigger goals and aspirations. The person directly responsible for training and motivating an employee is his immediate superior, and not the personnel manager or human resources manager.

I repeat: The people-management role is the responsibility of those people's managers. The human resources department must be a support service for department heads. It has an indirect responsibility that should always lead to direct responsibility, which resides with the heads of the various units. The objectives of the human resources function are the same as the overall business objectives: productivity, performance, financial standing, and so forth. Employee satisfaction is not a direct target of the human resources function.

There are no human-resource problems independent of business problems, or business problems independent of the flesh-and-blood people who perform the work. In business, people and business are inextricably linked.

> **People are important in business not because**
> **they are people, but because they are the business.**

Within other social institutions, a person has intrinsic value, but an employee has value because, without her, there can be no business. Business is performed by that employee, and losing her ability results in losing business capacity.

Part II

Diagnosing Incompetence: The Fougi Template

A Template for Diagnosing Incompetence

"He who seeks a friend without faults, remains friendless." (Turkish proverb)

"A medicine to cure all cures no one." (Unknown)

Learning to manage people is a difficult undertaking; even analytical people exhibit a general lack of structure when facing human performance issues. The lack of documentation, the shrinking scope of observation, having to judge by impressions, and the scarcity of structured models, often lead to settling for vague, unsupported conclusions such as: "This person is not working out; he has problems; he does not fit in; he isn't worth it."

Due to this lack of structure, it's seldom clear that you're firing a bad person and hiring a better one. While we can disagree on the severity of a disease and its precise treatment, we should be certain about who is sick and who is healthy, and the nature of their condition. Yet conclusive information on how a good diagnosis is performed and which solutions will work and which will not is often difficult to find.

If you deviate by 1 percent in a balance statement, it is indisputable that you are wrong. If you err in a production statement by 5 percent, or a general management statement by 10 percent, the result is certainly considered incorrect. But when it comes to people, exact measurements of their competence (or lack of) cannot be made, and any solution may be considered applicable.

You can never exaggerate the importance of a good diagnosis. It's ridiculous to eliminate the good employees and retain the bad, yet we often do exactly that, by applying the current remedy of choice—or the easiest remedy, which is certain to be the least appropriate.

A Misdiagnosis Can Kill a Patient

Both in business and in medicine, serious illnesses often begin with a previous misdiagnosis and counterproductive treatment. Besides missing the target, the wrong therapy can cause damage that did not exist before—the cure becoming worse than the disease.

When dealing with personnel matters, some errors in diagnosis stem from poor mental models. "Managing people is like salt and sugar," I once heard a newly-appointed human resources director say. Many managers define people-related problems with this kind of binary logic: If your work performance is poor, it's because either you don't want to work (lack of motivation), or you're incapable of doing the work (lack of skills).

If we limit ourselves to these diagnoses, we expose ourselves to the possibility of dismissing talented employees. Consider the third possibility that a worker may lack the resources or the proper training needed to do the job well. This may contribute to a motivational problem: The employee may not be motivated to attempt a job she cannot do well.

Thus, providing the training and resources needed to do a job are two fundamental responsibilities to which we may devote too little attention.

Main Incompetence: The Fougi Template

To help you make the correct diagnosis, I created the Fougi Template (Fougi from *Fourniés*—my collaborator on this model—and *Ginebra*), which contains 23 reasons why people don't do what they're told, which can be categorized into 10 different root causes and their corresponding corrective actions.

We want to improve diagnostic accuracy beyond the two basic diagnoses: employee apathy or employee incapability. And we also offer a repertoire of managerial remedies apart from the carrot-and-stick kind.

The 10 diagnoses are sorted from the mildest (irrelevant incompetence) to the most severe (incapability). We follow an algorithmic logic that eliminates the possibility of a mild illness before considering a more severe one. This complies with the reduction principle—that is, if an aspirin can cure it, forget chemotherapy. The template also uses what might be called the "apology principle." If an employee makes a mistake, it may be due to his lack of awareness of the correct course of action, not due to malicious intent.

The Fougi Questionnaire of Incompetence

Is the problem worth correcting?	No	Forget it
Yes		
Is the employee aware of it?	No	Warn
Yes		
Does the employee understand it?	No	Explain
Yes		
Does the employee know what needs to be done?	No	Give Ideas; Specify
Yes		
Does the employee know how to do it?	No	Train
Yes		
Is the employee capable of doing it?	No	Find Resources
Yes		
Can the employee benefit from it?	No	Consequence Management
Yes		
Is the employee having personal problems?	Yes	Support; Wait
No		
Is the employee willing?	No	Encourage; Correct
Yes		
Relocation		

Don't Sweat the Small Stuff

The employee whose faults are trivial...

Is the problem worth correcting?	No	Forget it

We diagnose as trivial issues those that are best left alone; errors that are irrelevant. Faced with minor faults, the most effective management action is to overlook them. There are a lot of problems not worth dealing with, because:

- They do not affect work results.
- They can't be fixed.
- The effort to correct them is not worth the potential improvement.

Confronting a fault is prudent if a possible solution is close at hand. Otherwise, it's counterproductive because the confrontation strains the relationship between the employee and the manager.

The longer an employee is in a position, the less it is worth attempting to change his basic personality. It is better to consider their traits as parameters of their abilities. "Bear your neighbor's wrongs patiently," is one of the Seven Spiritual Works of Mercy in the Catholic tradition. Bearing may also be more practical than correcting. A mature person knows how to tolerate imperfections and unpleasant circumstances. As we have said, we work among incompetent people, not perfect ones. We all have our faults and limitations, our bad days, and our awkward phases. We should not be shocked to witness this in ourselves or our co-workers.

Another reason to condone small mistakes is that a high percentage of them do not withstand the test of time. Their consequences dissolve in days, hours, or even minutes. There are flaws that seem intolerable at the moment yet resolve themselves or become irrelevant after some time passes. In hindsight, many problems are nothing more than amusing anecdotes. Those who forget quickly have an advantage here. I've seen ridiculous situations where a third party goes to great ends to resolve a problem that has already been forgotten by the original parties.

A culture of "excellence with zero defects" can create a choking environment when applied to employees. Fear of failure begins to dominate everything, and people inevitably feel discouraged when blemishes appear in their personnel files.

We live in a business environment sometimes prone to overreaction, where being five minutes late can lead to a 15-minute reprimand, and having dandruff on your shoulders or a dirty computer screen can be cause for reproach (I'm not making this up). A presentation of the brightest business solution may be seen as worthless if it fails to follow the corporate slide-show formula or has spelling errors. There are those who see problems where they do not exist, thereby creating problems that otherwise would never have existed.

Troubleshooting false problems creates real problems.

Labeling someone as a scatterbrain, or saying they lack focus on results, can actually cultivate that very quality in the person you criticized. It's like the Pygmalion effect: People internalize negative labels.

Don't confuse an occasional fault with an established trend. Spanish Judge Emilio Calatayud warns, "There are people who commit crimes and are not criminals. It is essential to differentiate this because, if you treat everyone as such, you'll end up turning them into criminals."

I invite you to overlook the faults of others and forget their mistakes, though this is an attitude contrary to our dominant perfectionist culture. If we want to build lasting relationships, we must learn to step over small mistakes, flaws, and misunderstandings. If we are not more tolerant, the list of grievances will grow, the gap will get wider, and interpersonal relationships will eventually die. Lotfi El-Ghandouri (2007) was right when he proposed his cynical self-dismissal concept. We start working with enthusiasm but gradually become disenchanted. We accumulate negative experiences and develop a victim mentality, and progressively reach a state of "self-dismissal," which almost always ends in actual dismissal. That is, we begin to say goodbye to ourselves as a prelude to being fired.

"A great man ought not to be little in his behavior. He ought never to pry too minutely into things, least of all in unpleasant matters. For, though it is important to know all, it is not necessary to know all about all. One ought to act in such cases with the generosity of a gentleman, conduct worthy of a gallant man. To overlook forms a large part of the work of ruling. Most things must be left unnoticed among relatives and friends, and even among enemies. All superfluity is annoying, especially in things that annoy. To keep hovering around the object of your annoyance is a kind of mania" (Gracián, 1647).

The Blissful Scatterbrain

The employee who is unaware of his incompetence...

Is the employee aware of it?	No	Warn

We may have an employee who does not perform well, yet comes to work every day cheerfully ignorant of his incompetence. His problem is in his blind spot; he can't see that his performance is lacking. In this case, the most effective management action would be to apprise him of the existence of a problem.

This flaw may seem minor, and certainly it is when compared to inability or unwillingness. How many performance issues can be corrected by one simple verbal warning, issued when the behavior first goes wrong? Sometimes we merely need to be timelier with our warnings, confronting a problem before it grows too large and while it is still a simple matter to remedy.

First we must warn the employee, make him aware of his incompetence, and remind him in very specific terms what is required of him; this conversation can be very effective in steering and modifying behavior. Sometimes employees spend months without receiving any guidance or feedback from their managers, without knowing whether they are doing well or badly. Perhaps this is because we tend to talk a lot *about* people but little *to* people. Candid feedback is especially critical during an employee's first few months on the job, when he is most likely to develop bad habits. Without monitoring and early correction, those habits will become entrenched.

The "blissful scatterbrain," the employee who is unaware of his poor performance, intends to do things right and therefore assumes he is doing them right, until there's evidence to the contrary. When such evidence is brought before him, he will most likely remedy his behavior quickly.

The Hyperactive, Short-Sighted Employee

The employee who doesn't understand his job...

Does the employee understand it?	No	Explain

Employees may perceive that something is not working, yet have no idea what they're doing wrong. The effective management action in this case is to explain. Stating how a job must be performed doesn't mean that it is understood, even if the employee doesn't give any sign that he is confused. The "hyperactive, short-sighted" employee often misinterprets his job description or misapplies his enthusiasm and ideas, to the offense of others.

We're all running too fast, and it is sometimes difficult to stop and explain tasks thoroughly. We expect employees to be already trained, to hit the ground running, and we're annoyed when we find out this is not always the case. If we expect an employee to seamlessly insert herself into a new role, we must be prepared to fully explain her responsibilities, and make ourselves available to answer her questions and monitor her early performance, as much as is necessary. This is one of a manager's top responsibilities, and should be painstakingly carried out.

Explaining a job is one of the key responsibilities of a manager.

Every professional must undergo a learning period, which has nothing to do with the short probation period provided in some work contracts. Perhaps we should hang an "in training" sign on those who are brand-new to the job.

We have to explain tasks in minute detail, because a particular activity at a particular company can't be known in detail by anyone new to the company. A general skill, such as running basic financial reports, is guaranteed to be applied somewhat differently at one company than it is at another. Managers shouldn't delegate their people's initial training, and should never think that just a formal welcome is enough; this only involves filling out forms, learning where the toilets are, and reading a huge folder of dry, irrelevant, and likely outdated materials.

There are many ready excuses to shake off the burden of explaining a job to newcomers. Knowing your work is expected, in particular for higher-level positions; yet when these positions are precisely the ones requiring a longer learning curve. You have to spend time with new hires, no matter how high up in the company they are and what their career experiences have been. Everyone, from the freshest college graduate to the most seasoned CEO, has a learning curve.

The popular situational leadership model of Paul Hersey and Ken Blanchard (1977) is based on learning and stresses the need for initial training. We have to treat newcomers as newcomers. Employees must be led to focus on the immediate reality still unknown to them, not only when starting in a company, but also when the company is undergoing changes.

Many managers, though they fully understand how to do the job for which they are hiring, lack training skills. They do not have a structured idea of the basic requirements of the job, the critical issues, major challenges, and key skills needed; they fail to translate this information into a language the new hire can understand. They have what we call "unconscious competence"—their particular skills and talents are engrained habits; it doesn't occur to them that there are steps, methods, and techniques that make up their particular skill that need to be spelled out for new hires who have not mastered it yet.

Explaining a job requires being able to describe in an orderly manner the precise sequence of activities. Explaining a job well also requires understanding and explaining the "implied" parts of a job: those unofficial, unwritten requirements that have as much or more importance as the well-documented requirements. This is especially important for the hyperactive, short-sighted employee, who has little or no intuition, and does not pick up on the unwritten rules that so strictly define his success in his job. It is up to the manager to make these unspoken parameters clear.

Reality is stranger than fiction. The dean of a business school kept ignoring the research aspect of my work. I could offer tons of suggestions and never get an answer from him. Whenever he asked me about objectives, or we defined them together, he would insist on course promotion, on sales. When I'd mention that my professional profile included research and that I felt he was ignoring it, he would deny it. But one day, he finally said: "I'm very interested in your research. You can conduct it whenever you want on weekends or evenings."

Explaining a job well is an art. It requires both a process orientation—the ability to clearly describe a sequenced set of instructions—as well as an intuitive grasp of whatever unspoken expectations there may be. The movie

Ratatouille contains an excellent example of explaining a job. It is during the scene when Colette introduces Linguini to cooking.

Colette's instructions to the "new hire":

- Keep your arms close to your body and your sleeves clean.
- Have sharp utensils; keep your arms in. You will minimize cuts.
- Keep your station clear!
- Cooks cut vegetables quickly, skillfully, and don't waste energy or time; every second counts!
- Always follow the recipe.
- How do you tell how good bread is without tasting it? Not the smell, not the look, but the sound of the crust. Listen.
- The only way to get the best produce is to have first pick of the day, and there are only two ways to get first pick. Grow it yourself, or bribe a grower.

The Theorist

The employee who has no real-world experience...

Does the employee know what needs to be done?	No	Give Ideas; Specify

Some people understand what a job theoretically entails; they could give a lecture on it yet have no understanding of how to do it in a real work environment. This is sometimes a result of being overly-trained in an academic setting, but painfully short on real-world experiences and what may be called "street smarts." A bank's branch manager may know that he needs to generate more loans and submit promising commercial plans, but he is clueless about how to actually do this. In this case, the effective management action is to give ideas and share experiences that will boost performance.

Specifying, clarifying, and suggesting ideas are tasks to which managers must devote a lot of effort. Specifying is highly effective. What is not specified is not carried out, and the more it is specified, the better it is carried out. Knowing how to specify makes a good manager stand out from the pack. Being specific gets you more results than being demanding. Managing people is not an abstract activity. Job tasks and responsibilities must not only be specific; they must be measurable, so that a manager can track performance.

Asking questions of employees about their specific, daily activities also results in better performance: How many report pages have you written? How many days will this project take? What points do you plan to address in the meeting? What was the outcome of your meeting? What task are you working on this afternoon?

> **A manager who is specific gets better results. And so does the manager who follows up on the specified tasks.**

In sports, we can observe the success of the management approach suggested above: When soccer teams play, their intention is not solely to win the game, but to score the first goal in the initial 15 minutes, make more shots between the goal posts, increase possession, or improve the conversion rate of opportunities. In psychology, we witness something similar called the Triplett effect: Runners try harder if they have to finish a lap in three minutes, than if they intend to run as many laps in the shortest time possible. Athletes and employees must have specific, measurable goals that they are motivated to achieve.

Ignatius of Loyola, in the sixteenth century, created the concept of Spiritual Exercises, which has survived to this day. After profound meditations on man's destiny and the punishments of hell, he suggested that practitioners set a small goal: a brief prayer, a small sacrifice, or a tiny act of service. Through these tiny self-improvement targets, he opined that we could ultimately gain access to heaven.

The problems of a people manager arise from a lack of detail rather than a lack of concepts. You can neither lead, nor can you go around the office giving strategic advice, without getting down to details. How dangerous are those managers who, when a subordinate asks for help, speak in general terms about creativity, motivation, and commitment?

Managing people also involves knowing the ins and outs of the business you're in: the approximate costs of running the business, project scheduling and milestones, competing brands, industry trends, new technology, and so forth. The generic business-management practices are of little use.

No amount of genius can replace the attention to detail.

It is necessary to recover specificity in the workplace. With specificity comes simplicity. We must avoid any jargoned, abstract language. Indeed, it is the same to talk about "strategic funding needs" as "funding needs," or making a "strategic social responsibility plan" as making a "social responsibility plan."

As Fourniés mentions, you may have a serious problem on your hands when the boss wants to see you the next day at 9 a.m. and you are not clear whether it means:

- Punch in at 9 a.m.
- Enter through the door of the building at 9 a.m.
- Enter the office at 9 a.m.
- Have coffee ready at 9 a.m.
- Enter the meeting room at 9 a.m.
- Be in the room with the slide projector on, already having reviewed the meeting agenda by 9 a.m.

Specificity and simplicity also guard against accountability issues. Vagueness gives people the chance to avoid being held accountable.

Be careful with expressions such as, "Somebody should do something about this." That kind of statement will soon be followed by this statement: "Nobody ever does anything around here."

Avoid these expressions often heard in the workplace that are the opposite of specific:

- "I'm on it."
- "I've thought of something."
- "Things are moving forward."
- "I've looked into it."
- "I'll be done one of these days."
- "I'm almost done."
- And all the known versions of "ASAP."

The Clumsy Employee

The employee who doesn't know what to do...

Does the employee know how to do it?	No	Train

Sometimes we confuse knowledge with know-how. Big mistake. It's like the average sports bar's football fans, who know how an offense is run and seem to think that, were they on the field, they would be able to perform it.

Our business environment is full of experts who are always preaching about how others should perform the work, though they themselves don't know how. They may have impressive titles, have attended conferences and read books, and may even have written them, but they can't put their theories into practice. There are people who write books on what they have learned in business, and others who think they know business by what they have learned in books.

One learns how to do by doing (and making mistakes).

So far, we have been speaking about incompetence related to perception and knowledge. We now introduce incompetence in practice.

We have said that to be able to explain, you need to know (have abstract knowledge); to be able to carry out, you need to know how (have specific knowledge); and finally, to be able to know how, it is essential to practice (have knowledge from experience).

The Importance of Training

Training is an essential function of a manager, and we are a little unwilling to practice it. It doesn't go well with our overvalued academic concepts, with our assumption that knowing a branch of knowledge immediately enables us to perform a task in that field. It would be nice if there were courses to teach any skill or quality: proactivity, creativity, patience, productivity, and so forth. Managers would be spared a lot of headaches. It would be like finding a pill to cure any illness. Unfortunately, such qualities can only be developed over time, although having a proper conceptual framework and knowing certain techniques may help us acquire them faster.

Micro-skills are little appreciated; generally we look for employees with broad skillsets—knowing how to sell, buy, inspect, or manage a business. Yet training is built on small skills—knowing the proper components of a speech, how to identify potential buyers, follow up after a sales pitch, make an offer, write an email, conduct Internet research, or use a specific software program. These micro-skills boost our everyday efficiency, slowly but surely helping us master bigger skills and competencies.

The practice of training is also an enemy of haste. Training takes time. We can't always check it off our list before lunch. Good habits and behaviors are only established over time; there are no shortcuts.

We have a skewed idea of learning:

- When we hear the word *training* we think about a course;

- When we hear the word *course* we think about a classroom;
- When we go to a classroom, we expect an agenda.
- We think that anything can be taught and learned in a classroom.

This is not a realistic picture of how learning occurs. Alternating concepts and practice is the best way to learn. Theory should be taught, and the opportunity to apply it back on the job and gain feedback should follow immediately. Time in the classroom should be short, but the opportunities for practical experience should be ongoing.

What We Call "Coaching" Is Not Training

Let's not confuse the training we advocate with the coaching that has become so popular lately. Although the term *coaching* is similar to *training*, it is not synonymous. A "coach" in the workplace is usually someone external to the company, hired to provide an individual with professional development advice.

The training we advocate is closer to the on-the-job training concept. The proper image would be that of a golfer's coach: someone who walks with the golfer, who watches how he holds the club, who corrects his swing, teaches him how to set up a strategy for each hole, and congratulates him when he does well.

I like to refer to proper training as "on-the-job coaching." The immediate manager is the natural coach. They have the opportunity to work closely with their employees on real business issues. They can teach the most appropriate and specific behavior, and detect exactly what goes wrong. Coaching requires formal dedication, known targets, increasingly complex challenges, and a clear timeline. Specific milestones in an employee's professional development are reached little by little.

Good training requires seldom-practiced virtues:

- patience
- discipline
- industriousness
- involvement
- humbleness
- allowances for mistakes.

Repetition is the foundation of any habit. Repeat, repeat, repeat. The extraordinary Croatian basketball player Drazen Petrovic would shoot 2,000 baskets every afternoon after school in his native Zagreb. And later, as a professional, he would stay for an hour after each workout to shoot 500 times.

Pat Etcheberry, a professional trainer of prominent personalities, tells the following anecdote: "Nick Faldo breathed golf. He was one of the most disciplined people I've ever coached. He would rise at dawn, and at 6 a.m. we were already working. Christmas came and we trained throughout the festivities, every day at 6 a.m. But the 31st came and shortly before midnight on New Year's Eve, I got a call from Nick. I thought he was calling me to tell me he wasn't showing up the next day, but he said: 'I'm going to ask you something, Pat. Can I come tomorrow at seven instead of six?' That was a first."

We must be convinced of the power of repetition. In the professional world, the more you rehearse, the better you can improvise. Repetition is the basis of learning, and it takes time and requires strong patience, both from the manager and from the employee. The organization also must have patience because new employees cannot begin contributing to it from the start. You can't accelerate the learning period if you don't want to run the risks of having insufficiently trained employees returning to their jobs. You have to plan and meet deadlines, lest you fall into a caricature of famous Spanish comedian Eugenio's joke: "God, give me patience... But right now!"

Here is a perfect example from a movie: Charles Chaplin's films, seemingly disjointed and full of improvisation, are the result of obsessive perfectionist zeal. Scenes were repeated up to 80 times. The famous scene in which Chaplin is filmed eating a shoe was repeated 62 times. Because the shoes were made of licorice, which is a strong laxative, the actor had diarrhea for a week.

Patience means allowing for mistakes, which are a gateway to learning. Workers and managers alike must have patience to endure incompetence without experiencing discouragement—without giving up.

Above all, perseverance and tolerance are essential in training, as Samuel Becket encouraged: "Try again. Fail again. Fail better," or painter Edouard Manet's statement: "When you've got it, you've got it. When you haven't, you begin again. All the rest is humbug." Mistakes must be looked upon as steps along the path to learning. We all know Thomas Alva Edison's words while developing the lightbulb: "I have not failed. I've just found 10,000 ways that won't work." And Jorge Luís Borges summed up the secret on how to be a writer: "Write a lot, correct a lot, tear up almost everything. And above all, don't rush into print."

Ultimately, the training process requires a humble attitude on the part of the teacher and the pupil. In my opinion, this is one of the major roadblocks to learning. We all consider ourselves wise, and have a hard time listening and learning. Winston Churchill said: "I'm always ready to learn, although I do not always like being taught."

A manager who teaches should not adopt an attitude of superiority, which would strain the relationship. Many managers compete with their employees; they feel psychologically compelled to demonstrate that they are more knowledgeable. But a good coach doesn't have to be better than the player. Tiger Woods's coach doesn't play better golf; however, he's an excellent teacher.

Recognizing yourself as competent is not the beginning of wisdom, but the door to ignorance, and vice versa. If a manager thinks he's superior, or an employee thinks he knows everything, it will end up preventing learning. If, however, the manager and the employee approach each other with humbleness, the training will result in enhanced capabilities and performance.

The Smothered Employee

The employee who doesn't have what he needs...

Is the employee capable of doing it?	No	Find Resources

If a worker has been properly selected and trained, yet still fails to perform up to standards, it is possible that he is incapable of doing so. Yet, more often than we think, employees aren't able to comply because they don't have enough time, resources, or support. If we have employees who are smothered by these circumstances, the solution is to get them the resources they need. On the other hand, if a properly-trained employee, who has never had performance problems, suddenly can't keep up, it seems clear that the person is not to blame, but the challenge, which is probably too ambitious.

You can do anything but not everything.

This is an important principle. We confuse the abstract ability to do anything with the concrete capacity to do everything at once. It is impossible to make 10 sales calls in one morning, or provide quality care to eight patients per hour. It is impossible to simultaneously monitor five projects in cities located 300 miles from each other, if their objectives are different, the consultants are rookies, and you have to devote time to their training; and meanwhile, you still have to collect ideas for a new service, prepare an article by a set date, submit a weekly report, answer your LinkedIn messages, keep up with the industry, accompany a colleague to a sales call, and prepare Christmas dinner... This is an actual case. You can guess how it turned out.

In our culture of growth, the targets we normally set stretch our energy, resources, and abilities to the maximum. We don't want to allow ourselves any slack, but in struggling to reach our goals, we suffer from burnout. Nobody wants to fall short, and the maximum achievable is taken as the most likely outcome. If a job *could* be finished in three days, the target will be to finish it in three days.

For tasks that are not measured by physical activity, the time we allot to complete them is judged inaccurately. Although it usually takes a two-hour meeting to build a business strategy, we aim to finish it in a half hour. Even though it may take us one week to prepare a document, and truly prepare it well, why not ask for it by tomorrow? The "faster, higher, stronger" Olympic attitude is detrimental when it comes to the everyday workplace.

We should go back to the cruise-speed concept, which is a pace that is neither a relaxed, enjoying-the-scenery type of stroll, nor a flat-out sprint. Surely you can go at a higher speed, but your career is an endurance race and you won't make it if you sprint your heart out all day, every day. We can increase our speed in short bursts, one hour per day, one day a week, one week a month, or a quarter each year, but we can't maintain it for most of the hours, days, weeks, and months.

Pressure Is Never a Real Solution

When facing a difficult target, you have two options: Stop and think about how more time or resources will allow you to do a better job; or join the race, despite the state of exhaustion you will surely be in when you finish. As the saying goes, "If you keep doing things as usual, don't expect different results."

Nothing burns employees and undermines a manager more than insisting on an impossible goal: demanding more without giving additional resources. Motivating your employees to perform to exceedingly difficult standards can backfire. You will lose their trust and support, and gain their resentment. Such behavior reminds me of a joke about a convict in a prison: "My horoscope today said I should see more people, go out and live a less secluded life," or that admonition of the apostle James: "Suppose you see a brother or sister who has no food or clothing, and you say, 'Good-bye and have a good day; stay warm and eat well,' but then you don't give that person any food or clothing. What good does that do?" (James 2: 15-17)

Achieving a lot under poor conditions is meritorious, although in the long run, you may end up paying a high price for it. As a manager, remember that you are on your employees' side. Don't walk away from their complaints. Make your employees' struggle for obtaining resources your own. The role of manager is to continually remove obstacles to allow them to work and achieve their full potential at a steady, sustainable rate.

Keep your finger on the pulse of your team's performance levels, what resources are available, and where the bottlenecks lie. Optimize work conditions, streamline processes, and eliminate unnecessary tasks. Managers are often reluctant to lower demands, reduce scopes, or relax deadlines. They fail to realize that focusing on a few priorities will bring them more long-term success than focusing on too many at once. When faced with an employee who cannot do what is asked, we should know how to say, "Don't focus now on those details; what we have is enough; actually, I don't need it until next week," and so forth.

Providing Resources Is a Manager's Key Responsibility

A manager has to be a resourceful person; one who in difficult times always has a backup plan: an idea, a contact, or information that unblocks the situation. In big organizations, there are many available resources, and the same goes for small businesses. If we look, we usually find that we already have the resources we need. The problem sometimes is not lack of resources; it's failing to undergo a thorough search for them.

For example, much information can be gotten from the Internet at little or no cost. Employees themselves are often overlooked resources. Company intranets often contain valuable organizational knowledge that everyone forgets is there. Some large companies even have entire departments dedicated to running numbers or studying issues at employees' requests. Perhaps all you can buy your employees is more time. This may be worth as much to them as state-of-the-art technology or top-of-the-line equipment: Lack of time is shown to be employees' greatest source of anxiety.

To be better people managers, we must obtain resources for our employees. Search and salvage, and leave no stone unturned in your search for the tools employees need to do their jobs well.

The Busy-Fool, Lazy-Employee Syndrome

The employee who doesn't think performing well is worth the trouble; and the employee who picks up the slack...

Can the employee benefit from it?	No	Consequence Management

Sometimes there are employees who have the knowledge, abilities, and resources to perform well, but it's not worth their while. They are not rewarded for performing well, and nothing bad will happen if they fail to perform. Meanwhile, there are other employees who work hard and constantly, yet end up paying a price for their labor. What kind of a manager rewards indolence and poor performance, and punishes hard work and excellent performance, you may ask? Unfortunately, these managers are out there—though they may not be aware of the disastrousness of this system they have implemented.

There are lazy employees who benefit from poor performance.

If your work lacks quality, if you shirk your responsibilities and disappear from sight at work, and if you complain about a task, the boss will assign you fewer duties. If you can't be trusted, and if you don't deliver work on time, they will leave you alone and you can live in peace. If you work little, and what little you do is done poorly, you won't have to face any challenging responsibilities, you'll be unsupervised, never corrected...you'll live in peace. If you are stubborn in your indolence yet exude confidence and "charisma," you can charm managers into allowing you to set your own work duties and deadlines. This kind of employee commonly chalks up a good standing among peers and enjoys the freedom to shirk his responsibilities without facing repercussions.

There are others who pick up the slack.

In the army they used to say, "If you ask, you'll get the next watch." If you perform well, most likely you'll get more work, you'll be the first one in and the last out. If you tackle the hardest tasks without a squeak, you'll be assigned the most sensitive issues at the most critical times. This kind of dedication is not always rewarded as it should be, but it *is* sometimes punished by overwork, stress, and more critical feedback.

An effective manager ensures that positive and negative behaviors are awarded and punished appropriately. This chart can help you determine if any of your employees fall into these categories in which behaviors are rewarded wrongly, and also to note how you think behaviors might be rewarded correctly.

	Positive Behaviors	Negative Behaviors
Positive Consequences		• Good schedule/less working hours • Easy tasks • Less stress • Left in peace
Negative Consequences	• Higher stress levels • Worse schedule/more working hours • Complicated, high-profile jobs • Putting out fires	

Cures for the Busy-Fool, Lazy-Employee Syndrome

First of all, you must ensure that actions have consequences. It often seems that no matter what happens, there are no consequences, either negative or positive; no feedback of any kind. Negative behaviors must be punished, not condoned—or worse, rewarded.

Sophisticated organizations have many requirements (regulations, procedures, protocol), yet nothing happens if they are bypassed, and it is tempting to do so. For example, to order office supplies an employee may be required to fill out a form, but he could just snatch them directly. Employees must be on time for meetings; however, they'll wait for everyone to be present before starting. We must punish this kind of behavior because it has more influence in setting performance standards than the official policies.

Reality is stranger than fiction. My 12-year-old daughter asked me one morning, "Were you ever kicked out of class in school?" I replied that I was. She added, "And where did they send you when you were kicked out?" "Home," I replied. Then she told me, "You got what you wanted for misbehaving."

Eliminating negative consequences for high performance is key to retaining talent. These kinds of employees are usually quiet people working behind the scenes, who never complain or push back. As a result, they are taken advantage of, and their work overload usually leads to stress, depression, and burnout.

You have to treat valuable, hard-working employees with special attention. Listen to them, seek their ideas and advice, and give them the recognition they deserve. Above all, be sure their workload is properly balanced. Require them to take breaks and time away from the office. Otherwise, they will disengage and leave the organization, or their burnout will lead to worse and worse performance. Either way, you are left only with the worst type of employee—the lazy, poor performer.

Learning to Punish Without Dismissing

Anyone in charge of people must learn how to reward without raising wages, and punish without having to dismiss. Our work environments today are sometimes too reliant on positive motivation. Just hearing the word *punishment* is cause for panic for both the speaker and the listener. Optimism, enthusiasm, and praise are simply easier to dole out than punishments. Negative messages are politically incorrect.

Leonardo da Vinci once said, "He who does not punish evil, commands it." Negative motivation (punishment) is an impressive force to guide behavior. Expectation of reward is delayed; the threat of punishment is effective immediately.

There are countless small actions that a manager can and should use as a stimulus for good behavior or performance (the word *stimulus* comes from Latin and means "thorn" or "spine"). Making someone aware of his bad performance is already an initial negative consequence. Correcting when necessary, increasing control, disclosing who is performing poorly, and publicizing the consequences of bad behaviors, are other possible strategies.

Ways of punishing (other than dismissal) include:

- stating what is wrong in an informal conversation
- using a formal performance review to communicate poor performance
- limiting an employee's autonomy and independence in his work
- assigning a less desirable responsibility or task to the offending employee
- eliminating benefits or perks.

If you lack inspiration, you can always look up Spanish Judge Emilio Calatayud's book of punishments. He sentences without resorting to fines and prison, instead seeking to teach a lesson. His punishments include finishing high school, learning how to read, or performing community service.

Learning to Reward Without Raising Wages

When it comes to rewards, the first thing that comes to mind is "salary candy." Money is seen as the ultimate motivator. However, resorting to financial reward is an expensive and short-term strategy. Spreading the good word about an employee, letting him know we have a good opinion of him, and making sure others know it, may have a greater effect than a cash bonus, which has little public dimension.

There are many emotional rewards that a manager can resort to: giving positive feedback, recognizing effort, thanking and congratulating. These rewards are simple, effective, fast, and usually cost nothing. A casual comment from a manager can have more motivational impact than an official recognition program.

Work environment, corporate culture, and individual responsibilities can also be made rewarding for employees. For example, assigning an employee to a project that aligns with her professional interests or goals, removing or delegating some "busy work," allowing casual clothing or the opportunity to work from home, providing useful tools to make the job easier...all these actions can result in a more satisfying, rewarding work experience for the employee who deserves it.

Ways of rewarding (other than raising wages) include:

- complimenting a job well done
- praising, acknowledging, and thanking
- making an employee's good work public
- assigning interesting and meaningful tasks and projects to the individuals who would appreciate them most
- encouraging participation
- showing that you value employees' ideas and opinions.

The Absent-Minded Employee

The employee who is suffering from personal problems...

Is the employee having personal problems?	Yes	Support; Wait

Poor job performance may be the result of issues outside the workplace. A worker who knows, is able, has the resources, is motivated, and has performed well thus far, begins to miss deadlines, deliver poor work, and lacks concentration and inspiration. When a worker is burdened by personal problems, the solution is to provide support, or simply wait.

Personal difficulties always have a strong impact on professional performance. We can't treat employees as if their personal lives didn't matter. The worker and the individual are the same, someone who brings problems from home to work and vice versa. We must break the barrier between the professional and the personal; the same person is on both sides of the fence. If you don't know what the employee is carrying in his head and his heart, you'll have a hard time engaging him in his work.

I am not saying that a manager must be worrying about or prying into the personal lives of his employees, other than under exceptional circumstances. It is simply about consideration: asking, keeping abreast of what's happening in their lives (if they offer the information), and keeping those things in mind. Something that takes little effort but could reap significant rewards. Think about who is in front of you, beyond what you demand of that person.

We should talk more about customizing people management. Pay attention to the motivations and interests that drive each employee. Perhaps one employee wants to be an entrepreneur, another an MBA, one wants to write a book, live peacefully, or spend more time with his children. What can you do at work to help them toward their goals, in a way that also boosts their performance?

There is talk of reconciliation between personal and professional lives as if they were separate worlds. We should rather speak about cross-contamination, both on the positive and the negative sides. Influence does exist—it is undeniable and inevitable. It is wrong to suppose that when we are at work we are only at work, and when we get home, we forget work. If your mother is ailing, your performance will change, and if the boss yells at you, you'll go home in a bad mood. We are not watertight compartments.

The trick is to learn, not to lose sight; to wait and try to align both sides of life as much as possible. A job that fails to satisfy the demands of family and personal life will not be sustainable in the long term.

The Unconfident Employee and the Deadbeat

The employees with motivational problems: the one who lacks confidence and the one who slacks off...

Is the employee willing?	No	Encourage; Correct

If we ask some managers to assess their employees, they will say that more than a third of them lack motivation and perform poorly. As we've seen, motivational problems are often misdiagnosed. The problem may be caused by lack of resources, poor training, some type of misunderstanding, or personal problems. Motivation as diagnosis is uncommon and rarely applied accurately, but it does exist.

We must distinguish two types of people lacking motivation: those who *can* perform well but don't want to, and those who believe they can't perform well. Of the former you must demand, the latter you must encourage. We must give positive motivation to those who think they can't (show the carrot) and negative motivation to those who can, but don't want to (show the stick).

We devote a later chapter to negative motivation. In this section, we discuss positive motivation for those employees who lack confidence in their abilities and underestimate their skills. They are the ones who get the blues when they encounter difficulties in their jobs or when they face a steep learning curve.

You must slowly build their confidence. Assure them that their doubts are normal, but that they can't use them as a reason to grind their work to a halt. Assure them that mistakes will be tolerated, even celebrated, as a stepping stone on the way to mastering a new skill or process.

Their past good performance and achievements must be emphasized. Praise and recognition can help to prevent motivational problems as well as cure them.

It is necessary that the person feels supported. Take him out to lunch. Just being heard provides relief. Reaffirm your confidence in him, and your appreciation of all he has contributed in the past. Tell him he will get over the hump and that he has talent, clarifying that he's only going through a learning phase.

The Incapable Employee

The employee who lacks the ability to do the job...

Relocation

We have reached the end of our repertoire of reasons for incompetence. We have exhausted the treatable causes (lacks knowledge, resources, or confidence, has personal problems, or has misunderstood the work), and yet the problem lingers. Now is the time to consider that the worker lacks the capability to do the job. The effective management solution will be then to dismiss or relocate.

Henry Fayol, the founder of the science of administration, argues that getting rid of those who are incapable is one of the eight basic precepts of good management (1915). James C. Hunter, in his book *The Servant*, tells the story of a famous Notre Dame football coach: "Holtz had a reputation as a specialist in building excitement in the teams he coached, and I don't mean just in the players, but in all his people: technicians, secretaries, assistants, even the water boys were always excited. Once a journalist asked him, 'How do you get all your people to be always so excited?' And Lou replied, 'Very easy, I fire those who are not.'"

This section may surprise some people. The majority of the book is spent defending the professional capacity of incompetent people, and now we are suggesting the expediency of getting rid of them. I recall the first day I introduced the Fougi Method to an audience: A participant approached me at the end to tell me, "So much complication, to end up firing people."

Although firing is an extreme decision, it is unfair to retain an employee who is not at the level he should be. Managing people requires foresight and the fortitude to not pass the buck on making those decisions that are hard and final.

Let's elaborate on this. Firing the incompetent person is a last resort. We must not diagnose incapability without having ruled out milder diagnoses beforehand.

> **It's better to retain an incapable person a little too long,**
> **than to part ways with a capable person too hastily.**

Before considering someone as incapable, certain evidence must be taken into account:

- He has been incapable for a long time.
- He has been incapable in various ways.
- He has been incapable under various managers.
- All other diagnoses have been ruled out.

With all these precautions, incapability would be a rare diagnosis. Less than 15 percent of employees are truly incapable. Going above this number systematically points to additional problems.

Differentiating Incapability From Incompetence

Don't confuse the problem-makers with incapable people, because we could end up wiping out all the talent. At one time or another, everyone has problems, and these can be especially acute in high-potential employees. It is essential to distinguish the performance factor from the potential factor.

	Low Performance	High Performance
High Potential	Problematic	Expert
Low Potential	Inability	Busywork

Professionals with the greatest potential often go through long failure-to-adapt periods, during which they exhibit poor performance. If we fail to see the difference between incapability and incompetence, and make a habit of getting rid of problematic people, we will lose promising individuals. Don't forget that the ugly duckling was actually a swan.

> **Getting rid of incapable people is not the same as firing those who are bothering you.**

The different ways people operate may be uncomfortable in the beginning. Some people are slower and others faster, some more analytical and others more intuitive; some are bold and some are safer, some go by the book while others are more spontaneous. Manners, work styles, and habits must not be punished merely because they are different. Such differences, instead of creating discord, can actually promote collaboration—if the manager has an open mind to having vastly different personalities on her team.

It's Not the Same to Relocate as to Fire

When an employee does not work out, we can find him another place. Closing this one door means opening other windows for him, inside or outside the organization. There should be a strong commitment to discovering what a person does especially well, which narrows down the responsibilities and tasks to be entrusted to her, ruling out the things she is incapable of doing. I was amused to read in an old ethics manual about the moral aspect of this quest to find one's own place:

"How many teachers hold chairs, or any work for that matter, due to the mere fact that it is a family tradition, or purely for financial reasons, without having the vocation or the ability to function effectively... This is immoral due to the serious consequences. For the individual in question: psychological imbalance, pain, lifelong failure; for the education of youth: he can't be efficient; for society itself: a real issue of fairness arises" (Marín, 2007).

Part III

Tools to Manage Incompetence

A Manager, a Teacher

"How do you go from being a track and field athlete to winning a medal in cycling? I'm a sponge; since I started biking late, I paid attention to every single advice I got. It was hard at first; I got elbowed, I had no idea how to position myself, I kept falling," says Leire Olaberría, bronze medal winner at the Beijing Olympics.

Every good manager must be a teacher in both senses of the term: a teacher as someone who knows, and a teacher as someone who knows how to teach.

A manager must be good at his job, be professional and possess technical competence. Ideally, formal authority must be preceded and accompanied by expertise. If you work better than I, from my point of view, you'll have authority. The day you're no longer able to teach something to those who depend on you, the day you stop surprising them, you will lose your credibility and authority as a manager.

Regardless of how much you emphasize the importance of attitude in leadership, it is undeniable that no one can be an effective leader if he fails to excel in his job functions, and if he does not know his trade. If we want to lead people in a company, it is essential to stand out in the trade or business of that company. You can't direct films without knowing about movies, or lead a band without having a good ear. That is why, for many years and to this date, engineers are primarily the ones who lead industrial management; account managers in advertising are usually very creative; chemists and pharmacologists hold key positions in the pharmaceutical industry; and computer companies are led by people who are talented with computers. Likewise, newspapers are often headed by prominent journalists.

Questionnaire: Do You Have Technical Expertise?

1. Can you knowledgeably discuss the major trends in your industry? What were the major developments in the last two years?

2. How many books about your specialty have you read? Do you subscribe to any industry magazines or other publications?

3. How do you learn about new findings? Do you have a strategy for keeping up? Do you have any colleagues with whom you discuss the latest developments?

4. Have you attended a conference or trade show in the last three years? Have you presented on the topic of your expertise? Have you traveled, preferably outside the country, in order to gain new experiences related to your job?

5. Do you know the thought-leaders and other prominent professionals who influence your business? Have you tried to contact them?

6. Do you belong to any social networks in your area of expertise?

7. Do your colleagues, both inside and outside the company, rely on your advice about issues beyond your duties?

How to Be Studious

It is essential to hone the virtue of *studiositas* that Thomas Aquinas speaks of, referring to a keen interest in seeking to know things (*Summa Theologica*, II-II, q. 166).

> **We often do things so fast that we don't stop to look
> at how we do them, and so learn nothing by doing them.**

Author Brian Tracy, a personal development guru, in his bestseller *Pathways Toward Personal Progress*, emphasizes the need to study, to see how things are done, and to try to improve constantly. There are many people who have not had a formal education but still exhibit a great desire to learn; they go where they can find knowledge, read about the topic, and ask questions. Here are some basic strategies to accelerate everyday learning:

1. Imitate a smart friend.
2. Seek advice.
3. Read, read, read.
4. Turn to the classics.
5. Seek out new tips.
6. "Sharpen your saw."

We will elaborate on each of these items.

1. Imitate a Smart Friend. "Mimic the one who knows" is the most basic and powerful formula to learn something fast. Skills are not learned by theory but by practice, and what is better practice than imitating the one who does it best?

Originality is overrated. It is assumed that every professional has to have his own innovative ideas; that's how he contributes more to the company. True, but if we look at business and financial history, we will see many great ideas that were formed by copying other ideas. Catalan Cava wine was born from copying the French and the famous Chicago pizza is also a copy. Almost all innovations in all fields have been developed through imitation.

After all the fuss accompanying the discovery of emotional intelligence, its main promoter, David Goleman, ends up proposing the same thing: "Among your acquaintances, look for models, especially [those] skilled in an emotional side that you lack, and imitate them. Imitate a smart friend. If you admire his self-control, and you are too emotional, copy his gestures, attitudes, and mannerisms. Imitation, repetition, and practice, not mere knowledge, will work better for you" (*La Vanguardia*, 1999).

2. Seek Advice. Seeking the advice of the wise is a fast track to learning. In classical ethics, asking for advice is essential to the virtue of prudence. And in the Catholic tradition, giving advice to those who need it is defined as an act of mercy.

Giving advice, seeking advice, and accepting advice, are not popular attitudes nowadays. We all feel amply prepared to be a source of advice for others. Asking for advice requires humility; giving it requires patience and objectivity. The one who knows everything does not need to take advice from anyone, and he who is going too fast doesn't have time to seek advice nor give it.

"To seek advice does not lessen greatness or argue incapacity. Without intelligence, either one's own or another's, true life is impossible. But many do not know that they do not know, and many think they know when they know nothing. Failings of the intelligence are incorrigible, since those who do not know, do not know themselves, and cannot therefore seek what they lack. Many would be wise if they did not think themselves wise" (Gracián, 1647).

3. Read, Read, Read. Most intelligent people are avid readers, especially in the business world. Both Steve Jobs (Apple's founder and former CEO) and Brian Tracy (prolific author, speaker, and entrepreneur) were loners in their school years and spent their time retreating into books. Carlos Andreu proposes to devote half an hour a day to reading a book on your topic of expertise (or what you want to be your topic of expertise). I take the following anecdote from the knowledge space of a large company where I once worked:

"David Vale from Atlanta wants to share this story: 'One night after midnight, another consultant and I were still at our client's office. I was working on a complex project that we were implementing, but I was curious to know what my colleague was doing. She was reading a technical book, self-training to expand her skills. And she did it while others slept! That is being disciplined. I'll never forget it.'"

Always go for the original work, not the copycat version. Great creators are much more persuasive than their commentators and summarizers. Each guild and each sector (from manufacturing perfumes, to growing vegetables, to graphic printing) have their bibles. These are the reference books that developed the key concepts on which the knowledge in their field hinges. Manuel Arias-Paz's manual establishes the basics for auto mechanics; Von Clausewitz writes on military strategy; those who study the art of rhetoric will always refer to Cicero; and cybernetics always turn to Ross Ashby's thoughts from his book *Design for a Brain*.

4. Turn to the Classics. You need to acquire a foundational knowledge of the profession you hope to master, and for this, you must turn to the classics. Go to the places where they excel on the subject: cooking in France, ceramic in Castellon, statistics in Madison, Wisconsin. Picasso, already a genius, moved to France and spent considerable time studying other great painters' works: *Las Meninas* by Velázquez, the *Dejeuner sur l'herbe* by Manet, and so forth. General Patton read the writings of Alexander the Great and of his enemy, General Rommel. Orson Welles learned to produce films by watching *Stagecoach* by John Ford 20 consecutive times.

5. Seek Out New Tips. Complex concepts, formal training, and expensive organizational learning projects often overlook the value of simple exchange of tips among peers. Listening to what your neighbor knows is an extremely valuable kind of knowledge sharing.

Today we can find courses on almost anything, but none may teach us that small tip that we really need. Sometimes it doesn't pay to attend formal training; it's not worth it. If you don't know, you're better off knowing who to ask. Informally sharing experiences will always be the best strategy for progressing quickly in our daily work. Share what works, warn against common mistakes, and learn the tips that lead to success, however small they may be. How can we achieve our larger goals without someone to show us how to access our voicemails on the new phones, where to find the staff list, or a specific technique for successfully pitching an idea to the boss?

I don't want to finish this section without paying some homage…

…To Martí Pich of Vitude, who showed me how to use Outlook's contacts menu feature.

…To a consultant at Improva who showed me how to reduce the number of pixels in all the pictures in a PowerPoint presentation in just two clicks.

…To a former human resources director at Pioneer Spain, who spent several weeks training his replacement, allowing her to learn existing procedures by sharing his experiences and ensuring a good transition.

6. "Sharpen Your Saw." Stephen Covey, in *The 7 Habits of Highly Effective People*, a mandatory reference book in the field of personal improvement, proposed sharpening your axe as the last of the essential habits. The logger who cuts the most wood is not the person who hacks the hardest and fastest, but the one who stops occasionally to sharpen his ax, so as to have more cutting power with less effort. Taking the time to sharpen your axe is essential if you wish to optimize your learning. You have to stop, think, and review how things are being done—the results that are being obtained. Assess your tools and your strategy continually, so that they do not become obsolete.

Imagine how much you can streamline your work if you discover quick ways to read and write, if you really master Word or Excel, if you are aware of the software solutions that are out there to help you do your job better! There are tips and resources to accelerate the most basic activities: ways of counting, drawing a diagram, basic writing techniques. A simple set of instructions, an archiving method, or knowing how to use Google's translator, can really boost our effectiveness. You also have to set aside time to review your methods, processes, and goals.

My Company, my School

Teaching is essential to being a good boss. Leading does not mean telling someone what to do and waiting to see what he accomplishes; it is in large part guiding him through the process. It would be very easy to simply engage in acquiring skills and then applying them to the job at hand, as if you were putting a puzzle together. But leading people requires a more hands-on approach, regardless of their level of education. You must train the employee on the skills you will expect him to know. This is the only way to grow in-house talent and goes beyond simply managing existing talent.

However, teaching is seldom found among the skills considered essential for leadership. No one records or even remembers the number of employees who have been promoted due to careful, continual training by a hands-on manager. Do we teach our managers how to teach? Do we choose them and promote them by this criterion? Or do we just promote employees who sell or produce the most?

Going from knowing, to knowing how to teach, is not easy. Knowing how to teach requires knowledge of the subject first and foremost. But many wise people totally lack the attitude and skills required for teaching their wisdom to others. Interestingly, we think people are very smart when we don't understand them at all.

We must look at the workspace as an educational space. Professor Rodrigo Uria comments on the role of education in law firms:

"The lack of teaching practices in university forces lawyers to have to learn our business on a day-to-day basis at the law firm. Law firms, large and small, medium or large, are true educational institutions that teach young law graduates how to become lawyers. A law firm that does not teach becomes a poorly developed, gloomy, bureaucratic group of legal analysts oblivious to the two cardinal functions of an attorney: counsel and the trial defense" (Roca i Junyent, 2007).

Medieval guilds were very aware of the necessity of education. The professional levels were:

- Master—master of the art or trade, and manager of the customers
- Journeyman—a professional expecting to become an independent master
- Apprentice—a student learning the trade from the master.

A person with a vocation for teaching is interested in knowledge, but above all in behavior and attitudes, and demands the best that each student can give. His technical skills are solid, but he also teaches more important life lessons.

> The people manager must teach the craft,
> as well as instill professionalism, independence,
> and inspiration in his employees.

An Approach to Teaching

José Ramón Pin named his book *To Lead Is to Educate*, to highlight the transformative role of the people manager. Here, we propose a concrete approach to teaching your employees:

1. Master the Technical Aspect of Your Business. You need to know the technical details of your business, and to master the techniques that make you excellent at your craft. We speak little about micro-skills, about the technical aspects of a job, about the craft associated with each position. Without mastery of and appreciation for these techniques, it is difficult to achieve excellence, and it is difficult to truly enjoy and take pride in your work.

We must understand each business in its concrete specificity. The heir of Cafés de Veracruz knew that in coffee, the most important thing is the process (of how it is harvested, cleaned, dried, and so forth), and that the raw material was less important. Olga Collazo, head of human resources at Venca (a business that sells fabrics by catalog) defined her company's specific skill as a thorough knowledge of fashion.

Each company has a unique customer base, brand, and assets, and a unique way to buy, sell, trade, hire, and strategize that should differentiate it from other competitors. We must grasp the critical points of our business. We often relegate the micro-skills, the specific tasks, and mastery of the techniques that make us good at we do, to the lower levels of the company.

Sociologist Richard Sennett, who was a professional cellist for years, describes his experience with vibrato as the basic technique for playing the cello:

"Vibrato is the rocking motion of the left hand on string, a movement that gives color to a note at its precise height; in vibrato, sound waves spread like ripples from a stone thrown into a pond. Vibrato begins at the elbow; the rocking motion starts from its fulcrum, passes through the forearm to the palm of the hand and finally is transmitted through the finger.

"The implicit ability of vibrato must be mastered before being able to tune. When young cellists fail to tune their instrument to perfection, every time they try to produce a vibrato, the note will sound harsh because it will accentuate the inaccuracy of the height and distort its harmonics; the precise height is our version of artistic truth in this discipline.

"I had a good ear...but it still took me several years to achieve a good vibrato. At age 12, when it finally came, the event set off a special time for me...This event was twofold: the respect earned from others by doing something well and the action to explore how to do something. It gives you satisfaction: by producing an exact and free sound, I experienced a profound pleasure in and of itself, as well as a sense of self-worth non-dependent on others' respect" (Sennett, 1998).

2. Develop a Taste for Work. Jorge Wasenberg, director of the Science Museum of Barcelona, claims that things are not fully learned until you develop a taste for them. And that taste is the best reward for learning.

By taste, we mean passion. An editor should have a passion for the written language, a graphic designer for art, a physical trainer for helping others lead healthy lifestyles. Today it is common to find apparel salespeople who dress poorly, booksellers who have no love for literature, and travel agents who are not interested in visiting the places they advertise.

Matador El Juli told the following story about his colleague, Paco Ojeda: "He had the best day of his life when, after killing six bulls, he left the ring, and do you know what he did to celebrate? He went to the marshes and practiced bullfighting all night long... He was a real bullfighter. Can you imagine asking a soccer player to celebrate by playing another game after winning the Cup?" (*La Vanguardia, La Contra*, 1999).

3. Commit to a Professional Vocation. Having a lifelong profession is not common these days. Career loyalty is almost a thing of the past. Etymologically, the word *trade*, in the sense of one's habitual business, meant "way, course, manner of life;" as in, my trade is my way, my course, the service that I must comply with in my job.

"Stability is a mandatory aspect of a profession; although not in itself immovable...usually, however, a profession is for life. It involves consecrating our whole human existence to it. A person who pursues one thing today and another tomorrow, without honing in on any specific activity, could not be called a professional in the proper sense of the word" (Marín, 2007).

We must recover the idea of vocation. Search for what you and each of your employees do really well; your natural talents. I don't advocate that people are predestined for a specific profession; experience shows us how chance, a good teacher, an enthusiastic friend, or family tradition determine a career. However, I do argue that each person has underlying qualities (artistic tendencies, entrepreneurial energy, rigor and discipline, desire for knowledge, empathy, and so forth) that naturally suit her to specific tasks in the workplace.

Many work in jobs that are not their vocations: educators working as salespeople; salespeople as managers; accountants as managers, and so forth. So it is not surprising to observe a general lack of professionalism: wine sellers who have no idea of the vintage; waiters in expensive restaurants who are not able to explain the dishes on the menu.

I see no other way to retain talent in the long term than with the idea of encouraging employees to pursue their vocations. Let each one do the work that he knows and likes the most. When you're in your place, you perform well (you are productive), you like what you do (you are intrinsically motivated), and you're useful to others (you want to serve them). All of these qualities benefit not just the individual employee, but the organization as well.

4. Set Principles. To teach, we must understand the concepts and structure of activities we are teaching and be able to make others understand. Wine-tasting is composed of three parts: Look at the wine, smell its aroma, and finally taste the wine. In the process of selling consulting services, you must understand how to execute the following: design and development of support materials; visibility and pre-sale operations; defining business objectives; service presentation; approach design; preparing a proposal; and finalizing the cooperation agreement. It helps to break concepts and activities down like this; learners will learn faster if they focus on one small action or one simple concept at a time.

To achieve professional excellence you must build a strong foundation. Before cooking a complex recipe, you have to learn the basic techniques: sauté, bake, fry. Without these techniques, you will have trouble following directions and storing what you have learned.

We need to return to the basics and learn the foundation of each trade. Here's an example of good practice: Musician Glenn Miller gave up a well-paid job in an orchestra to compose the music that made him part of music history, including such melodies as "Moonlight Serenade," and "Little Brown Jug," and his version of "In the Mood." Despite being married with children, he returned to practice piano with the patience of a beginner, and worked at night to create his unique arrangements.

5. Create Meaning in the Workplace. "Education is not the filling of a pail, but the lighting of a fire" (Wagensberg, 2006).

Show your employees the meaning of their daily tasks. Explain why they are doing them, how it contributes to the good of the organization, the community, or the world at large. Employees should have external motivation as well as intrinsic motivation. Professional ethics demand that we serve the customers' needs, not our needs—that we watch out for their best interest, not ours; this cannot end up being anything other than a mutually beneficial relationship.

An example of good practice: My friend and a great consultant, Andrés Merlino, carried out a project for a hotel chain. He asked waiters to tell him what their work entailed. They responded: Serve drinks or take the orders. Merlino helped them see that their real task was to bring happiness to people who visited a luxury establishment just a few days a year. And if they were impolite or had a bad attitude, they were missing the point. Their labor became more valuable and meaningful to them, and generated enthusiasm for their jobs.

Emphasizing duty, mission, performance, and service is the foundation of good leadership. A good boss should raise the sights of his employees to these four qualities. Joan Ginebra, in his book *El Liderazgo y La Acción*, analyzes these essential requirements for a leader:

- has magnanimous projects
- expresses plans, visions, and dreams
- conveys messages that inspire
- creates symbols
- gives meaning to the objectives
- appeals to shared values.

How to Become a Professor

To achieve excellence, we must spend time learning, and we must dedicate time to teaching:

- What time do I dedicate systematically to learning? One afternoon a week or one day every two weeks may be sufficient.
- What time do I dedicate to teaching? One day a week can be a good measure. Starting businesses may need more.
- Take time to observe the work of employees, just as a teacher reviews students' exercises, without punitive intent.
- Maintain an educational attitude in all management acts: Tell employees what needs to be done and why, communicate results, and gather lessons learned.

Two Additional Tips

1. Excel in a Specialty. Being a master in something specific is required. There should be something that you know more about than anyone else. It is more important to excel in something than the importance of what you excel in. It can be very ancillary disciplines with some relation to your usual work: database management, writing speeches, topical expertise, and so forth.

- What are the skills (directly related to my job or ancillary) that I excel in?
- What do I teach?
- What skills do I need to develop to master my work?

2. Develop a Curriculum for Each Employee. Develop a learning plan for each employee, a two-way table showing the skills that are being learned and the methods by which they are taught. I recommend forgetting the generic content (teaching leadership skills, time management, productivity, and so forth) and traditional formats; classes are merely one option among many. Instead, focus on specific skills that employees can use immediately in their unique roles. Let their offices be their classrooms. You will be their teacher.

Counsel the Doubtful

The act of scolding has frequent mention in the oldest moral texts in our history, from the Code of Hammurabi to the Torah, the Koran, and the Bible:

- "He who desires knowledge wishes to be scorned. He who rejects correction is a fool" (Proverbs 10).
- "Correction that admonishes gives life" (Wisdom 12).
- "It is better to hear the rebuke of the wise, than for a man to hear the song of fools" (Ecclesiastes 7).
- "For it [correction] will not hurt, but will heal under the guise of hurting" (Seneca, n.d.).

The English language has many words for the same action:

- Some have a softer tone: correct, admonish, warn, reprove, amend, reprimand.
- Others are harsher: scold, berate, castigate, cavil, censure, dress down, lay down the law, put down, recriminate, reprobate.
- And others are clearly pejorative: anger, enrage, nag, yell, fight, or alienate.

Correct (when used as a verb) comes etymologically from the Latin *coregere* (rule or govern with), and *reproach* comes from the Latin *opprobium* (shame, taunt). This variety of expressions conveys the many degrees of severity of a reprimand.

Correcting someone's behaviors is a significant undertaking that also harbors dangers. Reprimanding is a management tool with powerful effects, which can include significant damage. The mandate "counsel the doubtful" that heads this chapter has been defined by the Catholic tradition as one of the top seven Spiritual Works of Mercy. But conventional wisdom also warns that whoever tells the truth loses his friends.

Some have argued that a good manager must have perfect emotional stability, complete equanimity, without ups and downs, no matter what degree of bad behavior they are correcting (or degree of good behavior they are praising). However, we argue here that emotion can be an appropriate tool in an effective reprimand (or praise).

Correcting is a must for a manager.

We must know what to demand of our employees and how to do it, how to set difficult targets for them, and how to give negative feedback. Pusillanimity, indifference, and "goodism" are not part of a good leadership prototype. You are doing a disservice if you fail to tell your subordinates what they are doing wrong. However, keep in mind that a reprimand is a sharp instrument and should not be used carelessly.

Managing people complies so eminently with Teresa of Avila's expression: "Doing things right is more important than doing them." If you don't know how to reprimand well, it is preferable that you don't at all. As Aristotle says:

"The man who is angry at the right things and with the right people, and, further, as he ought, when he ought, and as long as he ought, is praised. Because that which should not be angry, or not as they

should, or when they should, or who should, appear senseless fools"
(Aristotle, n.d.).

Thanks for Punishing Me

As Seneca says, to correct is essential for the development of the person. So is correction not sometimes necessary?

Gracián warns us about becoming bad from sheer goodness, that is, by never getting into a temper: "Such men, without feelings, are scarcely to be considered men... It is a sign of good taste to combine bitter and sweet. All sweets is diet for children and fools. It is very bad to sink into such insensibility out of very goodness" (Gracián, 1647).

In our corporate culture, however, correction is eagerly avoided and therefore seldom practiced.

> **Reality is stranger than fiction.** For years I have been teaching a course on problem analysis in an executive MBA program. I make sure that students discover their reasoning shortcomings. Midway through the quarter, they are to provide a written report, which I correct sternly. On more than one occasion, I am asked for a personal interview, during which middle-aged executives will confess that never before have they been told what they were doing wrong.

A reprimand can demonstrate to an employee that he is worthy of your notice, that you value him, and that you believe he is too important to waste time on incorrect practices or behaviors. Tim Bell, CEO of Saatchi & Saatchi, used to feel ignored by the Saatchi brothers when he was not reprimanded. He said the less important you were, the less Charles Saatchi would yell at you, and the higher in the scale you were, the more you were exposed to his wrath. Maurice (Saatchi) had been the target of his bouts of rage, and Tim Bell was coming ever closer to this area (Fallon, 1989).

Receiving a scolding indicates that you are considered worthy of hearing the truth and able to change your behavior. IESE founder Antonio Valero knew how to scold to good purpose: People who had direct dealings with him remember how he would be yelling at them in the early afternoon, then enjoying a friendly dinner with him that same evening (IESE, 2007).

A senior member of IESE commented, "On one occasion, Antonio [Valero] asked about an issue I was responsible for, and I stated my concern regarding it. Valero did not get involved in the issue. He just told me, 'It's your responsibility. You'll see what to do. That's why you're a manager. If I had to make those decisions, I could manage IESE by myself with just a bunch of secretaries.' And he went back to what he was doing.

"It was the end of the day. I went home right away. On the way, I was assailed by angry thoughts. I was thinking of going in the next day and telling him he couldn't treat me like that, and handing him my resignation. I calmed down when I got home. The next day, he was extremely friendly with me. I realized then how right he was in what he said, and I changed my attitude. I will never forget that professional lesson that took less than a minute."

Discussing errors, talking about what's not working out, and listening to what may cause pain must not be considered negative, and we should not defend ourselves when it happens. Discovering one's faults through trial-and-error is one of the most effective ways to learn. "Errors awaken the ability to learn and numb self-esteem; successes numb the ability to learn and awaken self-esteem" (Wagensberg, 2006).

How to Give a Good Scolding

Correcting behavior will be helpful if we follow the Aristotelian principles of balance and the midpoint. Otherwise, the remedy is worse than the disease. The difference between a reprimand that burns and one that builds is in the details. A warning may do more harm than good because of the tone in which it is spoken, an unfortunate choice of words, or by disregarding the recipient's feelings.

Before you approach an employee with negative feedback, ask yourself:

- Is the issue worth correcting?
- Who needs to be reprimanded? (Is it really the employee, or is there another reason for the problem?)
- What is the purpose of the reprimand?

If you are certain that an employee deserves a reprimand, ask yourself:

- When is the best time?
- Where is the best place?
- How will you reprimand?

1. Is the issue worth correcting? Reprimanding is a harsh measure. The first condition for using it correctly is to have discarded other, less drastic measures. Follow the progressive measures outlined in our Fougi template. A light warning, a reminder, providing data that make a point to the employee, or a humorous note is enough to straighten out most mistakes. Structured sanctioning systems follow a logic process, from mild punishments to more severe ones.

I once heard a novice manager say: "Yell at the first person you run into, even if you don't know why, he would indeed know." This is not advisable. There must be proportionality between the force of the reprimand and severity of the problem. Few issues deserve a scolding. And, of course, scolding should not become a habit.

"There are men of gloomy character who regard everything as faulty... They condemn all: these for what they have done, those for what they will do. This indicates a nature worse than cruel, vile indeed. They accuse with such exaggeration that they make out of motes beams wherewith to force out the eyes. They are always taskmasters who could turn a paradise into a prison" (Gracián, 1647).

The reasons to perform a correction must be objective, not subjective; they must be depersonalized. Disproportionate scolding comes from inner anger. The boss comes into the office irritated for any reason and transfers his anger to an employee in the form of a scolding. The employee gets cranky and transfers his anger to a third party with a new scolding. And thus the anger spreads.

One way to judge the appropriate severity of a reprimand is by frequency. Correction is more appropriate after repeated errors. According to the Fougi principles, small, occasional failures should be forgotten.

> **Reality is stranger than fiction.** One morning, during an internal training program held on site at an organization, three people arrived 10 minutes late. The manager, who had arrived just in time, rudely reprimanded them, spending another 10 minutes doing it. When returning from lunch, however, the manager was over 15 minutes late, did not participate, and left before the training was over. A few days later, those employees left the company. No one forgot the scolding for being late.

What a relief when we learn to overlook occasional errors! And how regretful we feel after we explode over what turns out to be a minor problem! We feel worse about getting angry for no reason, than about failing to get angry for a good reason.

The severity of an error is marked by the consequences it has for the business, by its impact on others, or on the employee himself. An essential function of a scolding is to show the person concerned the serious consequences that result from his misconduct. The scolding then acquires an exemplary role. It sets a precedent for avoiding future errors.

2. Who needs to be reprimanded? It is said that Jack Welsh, when he was CEO at General Electric, gave a piece of his mind to a person he ran into at a photocopier and fired him on the spot. Later it was found that this person was an outside technician who had come to repair the machine.

> **We must reprimand the person who deserves it, and when he deserves it.**

How many times is the scolding given to the one who doesn't deserve it, because he happens to be at the wrong place at the wrong time, or to the person who is unable to defend himself? Sometimes we blame people simply because they accept the criticism quietly. In the words of Homer Simpson: "If something goes wrong at the nuclear plant, blame the guy who can't speak English."

Interestingly, there is a ping-pong effect caused by managers who, after giving insufficient instructions, leave the scene. After a while, they come back to check on the work and, predictably, they find that everything is done wrong. So the employee is scolded, the managers do the work themselves, and then leave the scene once more. This goes back and forth as many times as you like, with the same inefficiency on both sides. The intensity of the reprimand is inversely proportional to how well the manager explains the job and his dedication to training employees.

According to the Fougi method, first assess if the employee knows and understands what is asked, and whether he is able to change his performance or behavior. It is counterproductive to scold an employee for making a mistake that he would have avoided if only he knew how.

Cicero comments on the accuracy of diagnosing errors: "[The man] who, being free from anger, imposes upon each one the punishment that he merits. He will often let a man go free even after detecting his guilt. If regret for the act warrants fair hope, if he discerns that the sin does not issue from the inmost soul of the man, but, so to speak, is only skin-deep, he will grant him impunity, seeing that it will injure neither the recipient nor the giver. Sometimes he will ban great crimes less ruthlessly than small ones, if these, in the one case, were committed not in cruelty but in a moment of weakness, and, in the other, were instinct with secret, hidden, and long-practiced cunning. To two men guilty of the same offence he will mete out different punishment, if one sinned through carelessness, while the other intended to be wicked."

"When in doubt, abstain," would be a good standard when meting out a scolding or a punishment. It's better to risk not scolding whoever made the mistake, than unfairly scold the one who didn't.

3. What is the purpose of the reprimand? The goal of a good reprimand is to correct and educate.

Admonishing is also critical for maintaining social cohesion. Therefore, it doesn't come as a surprise that all institutionalized living communities (religious, spiritual, or political) have established internal procedures for correcting behaviors and actions.

The purpose of a reprimand may be technical (to correct poor work), or personal (to correct attitudes). There are two types of scolding: corrective and educational. Yet there is also poor performance that results from poor attitudes; the scolding this kind of behavior merits is reformative. It targets people with high technical capacity yet who fail to perform accordingly due to a bad disposition—those employees who know what to do and choose not to.

Procedural Issues of Scolding

A reprimand may fail, not because it is undeserved, but because of the way it is given.

1. When is the best time to reprimand? The reprimand must be well-timed. Scolding in the morning is not the same as in the afternoon, or after work hours. On Monday is not the same as on Friday. On one hand, it is important to not let too much time lapse between the misbehavior and its correction. If we wait until after a long holiday, the person may have forgotten her error, and the reprimand will feel like a slap in the face. It is sometimes best to reprimand on the fly, to ease the anticipation, and thus the tension, of the moment. One thing to keep in mind, if we decide to reprimand sooner rather than later, is that our anger or impatience may lead us to make a sharper reproach than is necessary. It's wise to wait at least until we cool down and can approach the situation calmly and rationally.

"Above all, punishing takes patience: knowing how to wait. Doing so shows a big heart. Never hurry, never get passionate. First be master over yourself if you would be master over others. You must pass through the circumference of time before arriving at the centre of opportunity. A wise reserve, seasons the aims and matures the means. Time's crutch effects more than the iron club of Hercules. God Himself chasteneth not with a rod but with time" (Gracián, 1647).

2. Where is the best place to reprimand? It is not the same to reprimand at the office as in the street, in a secluded place, or in a crowded bar, standing or sitting, with a drink or a table in between, over the phone or via email. We should aim to reprimand in private and praise in public. It is usually unnecessary to criticize an employee in front of his co-workers. He will end up feeling embarrassed and alienated—and probably resentful of you. A private, gently-worded reproach can disarm the employee to whom it is given; he is more likely to acknowledge his error without becoming defensive or resentful.

3. How will you reprimand? A reprimand should be well-prepared and supported by specific examples, and based on an accurate diagnosis. You may need to study the employee's performance over a substantial period of time, review his errors, and consult with others. A scolding should not be blurted out. Although sometimes we seize the opportunity to say something that we have spent a lot of time thinking about, any admonishment must have an argument, and this has to be prepared. It is not enough to say: "It's not going well." You have to structure a core argument that the problem exists and to which degree of seriousness. Clarify the harmful consequences of the error.

My mother-in-law has one of the best introductory expressions for a scolding: "I want to suggest something." And my friend Jordi Mir uses a paradoxical and wise expression: "I don't trust you, but I trust you enough to tell you that I don't trust you."

You must argue in specific terms, avoid generalization, and hold onto clear and indisputable facts. Your reprimand should leave no room for doubts or rebuttals. You must correct firmly and decisively. Reprimanding is a strong measure and to be effective, it must be applied without holding back. Go straight to the point, avoid beating around the bush, and above all don't attempt to soften the blow by praising the employee before you criticize her. Employees can see through this tactic, and the praise will come across as insincere.

Common advice for giving negative feedback usually insists on the need to correct behavior without belittling the person. However, you can still be firm. Scolding is less effective if administered too gently. The employee will not take the criticism seriously enough; he won't feel the appropriate sense of urgency in changing his ways.

Javier Fernández Aguado specifies behavior after an admonishment:

- Do not dwell on the mistake.

- Do not comment in public on what has gone wrong, let alone identify the person who made the error, directly or indirectly.

- Don't remind the employee of his error. No doubt, the person will have it present in his memory, and touching again on the same subject will only cause unnecessary pain.

- Recognize and praise efforts to correct the error.

- Do not doubt your employees' good intentions, until it has been proved that they are capable but unwilling to perform to standards.

Anger Makes You Lose Your Mind

The main enemy of an effective scolding is letting anger get the best of you. A heated scolding disqualifies the one the giving it, burns the recipient, and blurs the message. You can and should deliver a reprimand without raising your voice or striking the table. Harsh manners clash with pedagogical effectiveness. "Scream at a child," says Richard Boyatzis, "and you'll see how he gets blocked and won't be able to learn anything. But if you know how to relax the child, he will absorb your words like a sponge" (Amiguet, 2005).

You should deliver negative feedback calmly and rationally, and close the conversation with a gesture of trust, embodied in a plan for improvement. The employee should walk away knowing that you are confident that he can fix his mistake.

A good admonition is not incompatible with apology and trust, provided that both parties humbly approach each other. On the one hand, the employee must accept the reprimand without excuses, and avoid becoming defensive. On the other hand, the manager must not correct with an attitude of superiority. We all make mistakes.

A reprimand will be well-received when it happens in an environment of reciprocity. The boss should recognize some of his own failures and admit them to his team. A reprimand that has an element of reciprocity might include phrases like: "I could make the same mistake...," or "I used to do it that way..." If the boss never admits his mistakes, he will not have the authority to tell his employees what they do wrong. Responsibility is never one-sided. When an employee does something wrong, the boss is complicit because he could have been more careful commissioning the task and the employee.

Ken Blanchard, the renowned leadership expert, gives his view on scolding in the following interview published in the Spanish newspaper, *La Vanguardia*, in 2008:

How should a scolding be conducted? "No need to quarrel: talking is enough. Tell the associate who is failing: 'This is very rare in you: that's why I'm angry. If you did this all the time, I would not even bother talking to you.'"

Why like that exactly? "As you see, I complain, but at the same time, I am strengthening my faith in the bond, in the business, in the couple, in the son, in the person. The complaint must always be accompanied with hope for the other person."

Just like that? "I finish the talk, if it took a long time, with a summary and a review of the objectives we've set."

Why not replace him and move on? "I'm almost 70 years old and I have never been disappointed by people, but by their behaviors. If good people sometimes act badly it is not because they are bad, but because they have not been told what we expected of them, and often we don't even know what they expect from us."

And...? "The feedback, the response of others to every one of your actions, is the food of champions. But to eat, you have to ask for food. You must continually check with others about the effect of your actions.

Even if you think you know the answer, the very asking reinforces the bond and the expectations of each relationship."

Is that enough? "No, never take anything for granted: Speak clearly and agree on what each expects of the other. Create specific agreements, even if you assume they are convened. If, for example, he is afraid to be publicly criticized, tell him."

If it comes down to telling him that... "We are human and we can mess up anytime, but that does not mean we can't correct and prevent. Anticipate the attitudes and behaviors that bother you and express them. Most of the time a company's problems are ego-related. Company and ego are antonyms" (*La Vanguardia, La Contra*, 25-V-08).

Be a Grateful Manager

Thanking, praising, and congratulating are just as important for a manager to engage in as giving negative feedback and reprimanding. Do you show gratitude in your daily interactions with your employees?

- Do you send emails with the word "thanks" in the subject line?
- Do you ever drop by someone's office or make a phone call for the single purpose of thanking that person?
- Do you make frequent use of your organization's system for rewarding employees?
- Do you show your gratitude in other ways (a sincerely written note, lunch with your employee, a small personal gift)?

Have you been heard saying things like:

- Thank you for this idea; I had not thought of it.
- Thanks for being with us another year.
- Thanks for staying at work late to finish this.
- Thanks for coming in early today.
- Thanks for telling me what you think.
- Thanks for supporting me.
- Thanks for telling me what I am doing wrong.

Receiving praise is a human need; it is essential to forming nurturing relationships. How appreciative we are of thanks! I know a professional, over 40 years old, who keeps an envelope with all the written thank-you notes he has received in his career.

Thanks should be given to an individual for specific reasons.

To show gratitude, you must follow the Aristotelian principle of the midpoint. If you are always thanking everyone for anything, your gratitude will mean nothing. Commending for no reason, or for something not worth commending, is not really praising.

Thanking From the Heart

Gratitude must be authentic and personal. Some organizations have formal systems for rewarding employees, and they have their value, though when unaccompanied by warm personal appreciation from the immediate boss, the awards seem generic, a formality with little meaning or value.

It is sometimes difficult to thank because we value our efforts more than those of others. Usually, we think we deserve more than we deserve (and receive), and that other people deserve less than they're receiving. A grateful spirit reverses this trend. It downplays the self and highlights the efforts of others. "Our memory is singularly capricious; we easily forget the kindness we have received. However, how accurately we retain the memory of some lack of consideration, or a word that offended us. People easily forget good deeds over bad deeds. We are very crafty at reminding others about the services we have provided, or how hard it was to perform them!" (Chevrot, 2010).

Gratitude should be the capstone to any successful endeavor. It maintains peaceful, collaborative relationships, especially in the workplace. Being assigned a task and performing it well, and then being thanked for it, is a relationship-building process. It is mutually beneficial to the employee and the manager. From this perspective, it is interesting to discover that the word "market" is etymologically related to the word "mercy" (as it relates to grace, favor). In every commercial transaction, the buyer appreciates what he is given, and the seller must also be grateful for the opportunity to give, which derives for him a profit.

We depend on others much more than we know: parents, teachers, writers, friends, co-workers. We should especially know how to be thankful for difficult experiences or critical feedback—they help us learn and improve.

Thanks for Working With Me

It can be difficult to develop a habit of gratitude. We sometimes forget to thank those who help us in small ways, every day: the co-worker who always responds promptly to emails, the assistant who regularly anticipates our needs, the employee who buoys the team's morale with her own good attitude. As the poet says, "Be careful with those things that are forgotten because they are blatantly known."

As leaders, we must particularly acknowledge the work of our subordinates. We must recognize that our employees can perform critical skills that we cannot; that *they* could teach *us*. Our leadership is only effective to the extent that our employees grant it; our success is none other than the sum of the successes of others. It is difficult to be thankful because we sometimes forget what it means to work as a team and what it means to be the boss. The business culture in which we are immersed stresses individual merit, making things happen through your own efforts. And if we earn anything by ourselves, there is no need to give thanks. Yet in a team, no one can achieve his goals without the help of his team members. It is the false dilemma of whether the credit goes to the player who passes the ball, to the one who scored the goal, or to the coach. It is a game where the sum of the parts produces a positive result. Everyone achieves what they could not achieve individually. The thanking must be given, therefore, in all directions.

Managers must also remember that no one is forced to work for them; employment is voluntary, and therefore deserving of thanks. Josep Maria Feliu, after he took office as director of human resources at the Reial Automòbil Club of Catalunya, used to tell me very sincerely that the team he had was a luxury for him. How many bosses really think this way?

The alternative approach is to think that we are doing a favor to the employee; to believe they owe us the work, that they are bound to do it; it is they who are the lucky ones. This is the opposite of gratitude: This is condescension, and does not result in a mutually beneficial relationship, because there is no benefit to the employee beyond the salary he draws.

The main appreciation expected from a manager is the recognition of the quality and effectiveness of our work. We want to be praised for what we know how to do and what we accomplish at work.

> **Telling each employee what was achieved due**
> **to his work is the best way of saying thanks.**

Any good manager must recognize two or three valuable qualities in each employee and be able to name them in the same manner a team roster is recited right before a game: "We have the philosopher, the man with the original ideas, the one who is a numbers expert," and so forth. Publicly recognizing each other's unique talents and skills is a valuable teambuilding activity. Not only does it improve employee-manager relationships; it improves employee-employee relationships.

Thanking Strategies

Thanking is a habit and an attitude that must be engrained, and like any other habit, it can be developed through training. To improve, you must take concrete actions: give thanks to someone whom we normally do not thank; give thanks to someone who doesn't expect it; establish a few methods for thanking people and make it a regular task. Actions that may seem artificial or forced in the beginning will progressively become more spontaneous and natural.

- Written thanks: Stay away from formal documents issued within the standard protocol, as they are impersonal or overly formal. A simple handwritten note is most appreciated. If it is appropriate, when you thank an employee via email, copy your superior on the email. This way your employee knows that her achievement has been recognized in the highest levels of the organization.

- Verbal thanks over the telephone: Brief calls should be made for the single purpose of saying thank you. The thanks will seem less sincere and less meaningful if it is worked in among a number of new demands you are making of the employee. In the same vein, mixing praise and criticism in the same message can prove risky. Communicating something negative has three times the emotional impact than a positive message. Criticism always overrides praise.

- Face-to-face thanks: Nothing can match the sincerity of a face-to-face thank you. An effective physical thank you is specific, warm, and singular in its purpose. It can be given privately or publicly; whatever you believe the situation warrants. Each manager must develop their own ways of saying thank you. There are many possible styles, but some of the most sincere phrases include: "I couldn't have done it better;" I would have never thought of that;" I have not seen anything like this in a while;" "This is one of the best jobs I've seen;" and so forth.

- Rewards: Some companies implement formal recognition processes; but as we pointed out earlier in the chapter, anything that is formalized sometimes loses significance because it becomes depersonalized. However, this is one way of granting public recognition. It also officially increases an employee's professional value.

Gratitude leads to celebration, as its culminating expression. Celebrating is thanking explicitly, publicly, and in a festive manner. Celebrations of hard work and achievements not only grant instantaneous satisfaction, they also motivate employees to perform at an even higher level.

Forgive, Greet, and Say Please

Greeting, saying "please," apologizing, and forgiving, are the final actions for effective management that we will discuss. These actions are gestures of respect, strengthening the relationship between manager and employee. When these basic rules of social interactions are broken, the most fruitful professional relationships can be destroyed. Have you ever witnessed partners, colleagues, and friends who throw away years of camaraderie due to a failure to apologize and forgive?

We want our work interactions to be more than just an exchange of labor. Though they are professional relationships, they can be deeply personal as well. Anthropologist Marshall Sahlins describes this idea in his book *Tribesmen*:

"In an uncommon number of tribal transactions, material utility is played down, to the extent that the main advantages appear to be social, the gain coming in good relations rather than in good things. I refer to the many varieties of reciprocal 'gift-giving' (so-called), ranging from informal hospitality to the formal exchanges that seal a marriage or a blood-brotherhood. These are instrumental exchanges;

they establish solidarity between people through the instrumentality of things (as we say, but on relatively rare occasions, it is the feeling that counts). In these transactions, the parties may exchange some of the goods available to each. Sometimes, when establishing a blood-brotherhood, settling an argument or arranging a marriage, people give each other equal amounts of identical goods. Is it a waste of time and effort...? The purpose was morale. The purpose of the exchange was to generate a friendly feeling between the two people involved, and if this is not achieved, the purpose was unsuccessful. The purpose is peace" (Sahlins, 1968).

To build a meaningful, rewarding professional relationship, you must value your employees beyond their basic utility. There are small emotional levers you can pull to signal your respect.

When assigning a task or making a request:

- Greet the employee.
- Say "please."

After the task is completed:

- When done well, thank and congratulate.
- When done poorly, apologize and forgive.

The Greeting

Greeting is the first step in an emotionally healthy interaction. Greetings should be frequent; at the start of the day, at the beginning of the year or quarter, after the holidays, or whenever there is a relocation of positions and responsibilities.

A careless, gloomy, or impatient greeting can affect an employee's mood and performance. He may be reluctant to approach you with questions or concerns, believing that you're in a bad mood; or he may wonder what he did to upset you. Greeting is the most basic sign of recognition and trust. Failing to greet someone is failing to meet the minimum requirement for a relationship.

A greeting also creates interpersonal space. It means you are entering to occupy the same place (a room, office, or company). Saying good-bye is the complementary action; it is declaring that you are no longer in the same environment. Saying hello and good-bye means acknowledging each other.

The worst thing you can say about a manager, or anyone else, is that he does not say hello or good-bye. It is living like strangers, ignoring each other. And indeed, there are bosses who never say hello or good-bye. This is hard to believe, but in larger organizations, even though their offices may be nearby, an employee may not see her manager for days, unless they happen to pass in the hallway.

> **Reality is always stranger than fiction.** For a year, I had a boss who did not greet me even once. I saw him at our introductory meeting, which lasted seven minutes, then we communicated by phone or email very occasionally. One day, we received an email stating that he was no longer our manager.

When a manager stops saying hello, or reduces it to a careless formality, he is expressing that the relationship is degraded. By contrast, when a manager values his people, he will first show it in the way he greets others. Greeting is more than just saying good morning. It's making yourself available, being within reach. Greeting someone lets her know that you are close at hand and ready to help.

In urban business environments, it is sometimes difficult to say hello. The general atmosphere is one of impersonal seriousness. The do-not-intrude or do-not-waste-my-time mentality is what governs. Greeting and being greeted is considered bothersome. In other contexts, however, we are better greeters: on a summer outing, at a social gathering, or at a place of worship.

Pay attention to how and whom you greet. Greeting your employees doesn't have to mean you waste a whole day talking about sports or joking around. Often a smile will suffice.

Ask yourself these questions:

- Do I habitually greet my employees and co-workers?
- Are there people important to my job whom I don't greet for long periods of time?
- Do I make a point of greeting people after a long absence?
- Do I have time to say good-bye before leaving for the night?
- Do I arrive at a meeting or event in time to greet everyone present? Or do I arrive just in time for the meeting to officially begin?
- Are my greetings friendly and personal? Or are they rushed and formal?

Please Say "Please"

Another critical element of a healthy work interaction is to say "please" when asking for something. A request can be issued in various forms, and how it is issued will affect how the work is performed. Commanding is not the same as asking. The boss dictates what to do, and the employee gets to it because he has no choice, because he has to, because it is his duty, because it says so in the contract, and because he receives a salary in exchange. It is the traditional attitude of command-and-control, or the simple commercial attitude of fulfilling the agreement. Everything comes down to orders or commitments. Nobody does or receives favors from anyone.

The boss who asks the employee by saying "please" implies that the work is appreciated and that the employee does have a choice in completing the work. It signals that the manager respects the employee's time and abilities, and doesn't take him for granted. Saying "please" also signals that you trust the employee and that you consider him competent.

Here are some phrases you might use when assigning a task in a way that shows your employees you respect and value their contribution:

- Could you see if...?
- Would you mind...?
- How do you feel about…?
- The ball is in your court; just let me know if you need help.

Framing your request in these words allows the employee to voice her suggestions or concerns before beginning the task. Also interesting is the formula used by renowned psychologist Victor Frankl; when Alex Pattakos consulted him on his intention of writing a book about applying his ideas to the world of work: "It is a necessary book. Fulfill your mission."

On Apologizing and Forgiving

Forgiveness can be one of the most difficult, yet most critical, actions for a manager. If a reprimand corrects a behavior at the objective level, forgiving corrects at the emotional level. If the thanking reinforces the work relationship when things go right, reconciling strengthens the relationship when they don't.

The reconciliation process has two components: first, the wrong-doer apologizes, and then the affected party forgives. Because it is for the victim to forgive and for the offender to apologize, we would prefer to be the former. Apologizing is humiliating. It means recognizing and publicly acknowledging that we have acted wrongly. Apologizing is recognizing our own incompetence, and admitting that we didn't know enough, or that we lacked skill, initiative, or resilience. Forgiveness seems to belong to the superior, and apologizing to the subordinate.

Apologizing is different from making excuses, but the difference is subtle. When a person apologizes, he recognizes his own responsibility and admits the blame. When a person makes excuses, the opposite happens: The responsibility is placed elsewhere. He transfers the blame to external factors: circumstances, third parties, and so forth.

Against his instincts, a good leader must learn, and get used to, apologizing. Managers seem to be pressured, mainly for the sake of maintaining the organization's public image, into never admitting errors. We think that acknowledging mistakes damages our credibility and authority, but even more damaging is refusing to acknowledge failures that are obvious to all.

In the long run, all personal relationships are at some point reconciled or broken. Adult relationships are maintained by forgiveness. If you don't forgive, breaking up is inevitable. However, forgiveness is not easy. "Write offenses on sand and gratitude in stone," is a good rule to form healthy personal relationships, though we often follow the opposite strategy. Seneca speaks about those who are better at getting angry than forgiving: "How often do we hear: This cannot be tolerated! It is unforgivable! We tend to magnify the mistakes of others and minimize ours" (Seneca, n.d.).

We usually begin relationships giving the other person the benefit of the doubt, but over time we allow misunderstandings, small injustices, grievances, moody moments, and so forth, to accumulate and chip away at the bonds. Each misunderstanding is a turning point and, if badly handled, drives you apart. However, forgiveness can bring you closer. The point is not to avoid conflict, as it is inevitable, but to know how to overcome it. According to Psychologist Bruce Tuckman (1965), team relationships necessarily involve the successive stages of "forming, storming, norming and performing." We can only achieve consolidation after overcoming stormy times.

Forgiveness can also pave the way for learning. If a task poorly handled leads to a loss of confidence in the employee, apologizing rebuilds that confidence at a deeper level. Georges Chevrot advises, "When it is hard for us to forgive, we should ask ourselves, wouldn't it be convenient for others to be forgiving with us? How many times has the one asking for forgiveness been denied it?" (Chevrot, 2010)

Apologizing lets others know that we can do better. Forgiving is acknowledging that the other person can do better. It is betting on the future, and distancing ourselves from the mistake. Forgiveness feeds on the principle of apology, on the willingness to see the positive side of the employee and downplay the negative. It is giving the employee the benefit of the doubt.

Sometimes it's best to attribute errors to causes beyond the employee: He was unlucky; the circumstances were adverse. But when your employee succeeds, chalk it up to him: He knows a lot; he is an excellent employee; he always does the best he can. The manager who thinks this way attracts employees; he is receptive because when you approach him, he raises your value; your strengths are increased and weaknesses reduced. At the other end, we find the repellent manager: When you approach him, your qualities are decreased and your flaws increased.

A repellent manager thinks according to the inference scale. He looks at the negative side, and interprets the data in the worst way. He considers faults to be entrenched; he is suspicious and constantly critical of employees because he believes that their intentions are bad.

The receptive manager carries the blame, minimizes the bad, and distributes the good, as expressed by Fernández Aguado. The repellent manager blames; he downplays the good and spreads the bad. The receptive manager allows mistakes because mistakes do not impair the professional relationship. Thus, he launches the final phase of the forgiveness process: Let's get back to working together with a good attitude.

Humberto Maturana uses this idea as part of his peculiar concept of business biology. He discussed it in this interview for *La Vanguardia,* published in 2005:

"I remember the CEO of a Chilean pharmaceutical company whose executives forced him to launch an investigation to find the culprit of a labeling error and fire him. It was either the employee or himself."

What did you advise him? "Not to be a cop, but to be a businessman and forget about looking for the culprits, but find out the reasons. If he kept looking for culprits, everyone would lie for fear of being fired, and perhaps he would end up firing an employee while the error would remain. However, if he asked for help to find the causes, he would find support and then the causes."

Did he get the support? "He found out that the error had occurred as a result of the managers' request to increase production."

Did he fire anyone? Why? "The cause of the error was corrected. The employees apologized with honesty and returned to work in a different way because they had been relied upon. And the effect is systemic: if you punish the error, the next person hides behind a lie, while the mistake is not corrected; whereas, if you respect the mistake, you can correct it and increase everyone's responsibility. Try it with children. You'll see" (*La Vanguardia, La Contra,* 07-XI-05).

Conclusion: I Know Only That I Know Nothing

We have reached the end of our journey. Thanks for walking with me all this way, but I have to admit that I couldn't get enough. I hope the same is true for you.

As in the best debates, many issues remain open in both breadth and depth. Most of the book remains to be written. I have deleted many sections, which I hope to incorporate into a future version. However, I do want to emphasize an overall conclusion that has appeared repeatedly in the text, at times implicitly, at other times more explicitly:

> **Humbleness is an essential management skill,**
> **especially in regard to managing people.**

We have seen how arrogance blocks the educational function, prevents reprimands from being performed correctly, and removes forgiveness and appreciation from employee relations. In fact, there is a formula to define management talent that incorporates arrogance as its core element.

Executive talent = Talent you have / Talent you think you have

Effective managerial talent is directly proportional to potential professional talent, but inversely proportional to the size of the ego. A person worth 100, who thinks he's worth 120, has less value than a person who is worth 80 and thinks he's worth 70.

To increase managerial talent, professional talent must also be increased (an activity that we usually put a lot of effort into) but the ego should also be reduced (an activity we usually do not put a lot of effort into). When a manager's arrogance grows faster than his professional capacity, his managerial talent decreases dramatically. Arrogance makes us more vulnerable, while the recognition of one's incompetence makes us stronger. This is the focus of our discourse, the Socratic "I know only that I know nothing," as the foundation of wisdom, learning, and building good relationships with employees.

Managers are wrong when they insist on stressing their professional strengths to their teams. Employees may not have the same opinion of them. The perfect manager drives away his employees. He fails to be welcoming because he leaves no room for anyone else. By being perfect, he doesn't need anything or anyone. As Moebius says, "Error and imperfection allow us to open ourselves to change and meet others, because intellectual, physical strength, and seduction build a wall and leave others outside. The strong one can only be saved by a hole in that wall."

All this points to the discovery of a new management model, the concept of a peaceful manager, which I have discussed in other places: a manager who knows how to wait, who doesn't pretend to be unbeatable or the greatest. He tries to be just good enough, and adapts his talents to the situation. He doesn't pretend to have all the answers and avoids at all costs seeming too smart, in favor of nurturing good relationships with others.

Again, we return to the paradox that has presided over this book. Effective managers are those who acknowledge their incompetence. We win people by being reasonable and lose them by being extraordinary. This type of approach should be our driving force.

A good essay always sparks a thought process that does not end when the essay must unavoidably be edited (from the Greek verb meaning *to cut*). It is always a work in progress, under constant review and never final. I hope to have opened a debate among my readers, as I have with my students at the company, and at the university where I have presented this content. They have provided me with criticism, comments, congratulations, experiences, applications, and even terms for christening the types of incompetent people.

Permanent dialog, a community of debate, is now more possible than ever with the emergence of the Internet. Thus, I invite you to visit my blog: http://gestiondeincompetentes.com/.

And to follow me by using tools such as LinkedIn. Like the pirate's song goes: "I'm only singing my song to the one who sails with me."

Appendix:
Twenty-Five Incompetent
Characters in Films

We live in the era of cinema and visual media. In my living room, DVDs are beginning to stack up and hide my books; there is nothing like a good film to convey attitudes and behaviors.

There's a lot we can learn from movie plots and characters when we are performing our jobs as managers. If the reader has the drive to see and hear, and is willing to learn from three or four of the movies listed below, I would think that the benefits of this book would be tenfold.

THE CHORUS (Work with what you have)
Original title: Les choristes
Director: Christophe Barratier
Cast: Gérard Jugnot, François Berleand, Kad Merad
Country: France
Year: 2004

A rich and famous musician is visited by his first music teacher, and together they begin to remember old times. Clément Mathieu used to teach music at a rural orphanage, and he thought he had discovered talent among some of the children. Against the authoritarian ways of the director of the center, he insisted on trusting the children, who were continually threatening to betray that trust. With overwhelming patience, he formed a choir that ended up performing successfully before the local authorities. It is hard to find such graphic examples of betting on the people you have and striving to avoid disqualification; taking on a paternal role, and seeing possibilities even in things that are normally ignored.

Mathieu demands, corrects, encourages, gives resources, establishes procedures, trains, and makes everyone work hard. He finally manages to develop exceptional musical qualities in one of the orphans. And for all the children, this is a chance to strive to learn, undergo discipline, and be involved in something worthwhile.

THE DIRTY DOZEN (Work with what you have; Teaching how to work)
Original title: The Dirty Dozen
Director: Robert Aldrich
Cast: Lee Marvin, Ernest Borgnine, Charles Bronson
Country: USA
Year: 1967

This is a classic war movie often used in training programs. During the second World War, 12 military prisoners with death sentences or life terms are recruited to carry out a daring mission behind enemy lines. An officer trains them, listens to them, and punishes them when necessary, trying to achieve effective results from this bunch of goofs he has to deal with.

Can he be successful with his mission?

With endless patience, he makes use of all the management tools: he threatens and rewards, teaches techniques, provides resources, poses challenges, and gives incentives that foster collaboration and create a team spirit.

He also performs a detailed person-by-person analysis and evaluation and has to deal with both internal and external conflicts.

BABE (Work with what you have; Teaching how to work)
Original title: Babe
Director: Chris Noonan
Cast: James Cromwell, Magda Szubanski
Country: Australia
Year: 1995

A farmer wins a piglet at a local fair but his favorite sheepdog is not feeling well. On the farmer's intuition, Babe (the pig) takes on a career as a sheepherding dog (pig). His family thinks it's crazy. After arduous training involving different animals, he enters a county contest and wins.

All the big issues of professional growth are reflected in a very graphic way: perseverance in training, asking for advice, and creating communication strategies and tactics. Ultimately the boss' stubbornness in believing in the talent of his "people" makes them capable of being anything they want to be.

HOOSIERS (Work with what you have; Counsel the doubtful; Thanking and congratulating)
Original title: Hoosiers
Director: David Anspaugh
Cast: Gene Hackman, Barbara Hershey
Country: USA
Year: 1986

Norman Dale goes to Indiana to coach a small-town high school basketball team for a year. Few students sign up, the star player is suffering from depression and doesn't want to participate, and the team record is bleak. Norman embarks on a team-building process, which will lead the team from Hickory on a historic run for the state championship (based on a true story).

Throughout the season, he uses lots of management resources: issues guidelines, punishes selfishness on the court, learns from the games. Depending on the talent of each player and the degree of maturity of the team, he progressively changes his management style. At the same time, he also undergoes a professional transformation and utilizes a former trainer, helping him overcome alcoholism.

JERRY MAGUIRE (Work with what you have; Training)
Original title: Jerry Maguire
Director: Cameron Crowe
Cast: Tom Cruise, Cuba Gooding Jr.
Country: USA
Year: 1996

The lead character is fired from a sports agency for suggesting that having too many clients leads to poor service. Everyone supports his ideas initially, but nobody follows through. He is left with only a secretary, one client, and a fish to take on his new venture.

The difficulties of managing people are clearly shown in this film: the importance of family, self-esteem problems, using strong tools (scolding) to deal with certain attitudes, persuasion, a combination of a soft and hard approach, communication, and putting yourself in the other person's shoes.

THE HUDSUCKER PROXY (Acknowledging your own incompetence)
Original title: The Hudsucker Proxy
Director: Joel Coen
Cast: Tim Robbins, Jennifer Jason Leigh, Paul Newman
Country: USA
Year: 1994

Norville Barnes is a naïve and simple-minded young man from a small town, who comes to the city looking for a job to start his career. He starts as a mailroom worker at a hugely successful corporation at the same time as the head and main shareholder of the company commits suicide by jumping off a balcony. The directors concoct a scheme to make the stock fall low enough and then buy it up for pennies on the dollar by appointing a moron to run the company. However, things do not go as planned.

This exceptional comedy by the Coen Brothers goes over several business processes: logistics, pricing, accounting, point of sale, and so on, and reflects issues on professional competence and incompetence. Barnes finally has a moment of inspiration and invents the Hoola-Hoop, which ends up being the biggest business success at the time, driving up the stock price, to the despair of the board members.

THE BOSS OF IT ALL (Incompetent bosses)
Original title: Direktøren for det hele Lars Von Trier
Cast: Jens Albinus, Peter Gantzler, Louise Mieritz
Country: Denmark
Year: 2006

A business owner has refused explicitly to work as the manager, and for years he has simulated the existence of a ghost manager whom nobody has ever seen. Now he wants to sell, and buyers demand to know the manager in person. So he hires an actor to play the role.

The film is a satire on the manager's image. The actor discovers in his own flesh, the duties, methods, and relationship styles, of that ghost boss whom he now embodies. Fact and fiction mixed up as never before.

THE DEVIL WEARS PRADA (Incompetent bosses; Work-life balance)
Original title: The Devil Wears Prada
Director: David Frankel
Cast: Meryl Streep, Anne Hathaway, Stanley Tucci, Emily Blunt
Country: USA
Year: 2006

The title clearly sets the tone of this film about Miranda Priestly, the director of the most important fashion magazine in the country. But this movie is far from a caricature on how manipulative managers can be. The director has thoroughly studied the intricacies of the industry and its organizations, and gives a very real picture of the pace of work, how to be organized, and the world of public relations.

In fact, the lead character is not Miranda but Andy Sachs, her assistant who has a curious love-hate relationship with her boss. Through Andy's eyes, the film raises issues such as conciliating working life and personal life, competition among co-workers, and industry knowledge.

Gradually, Miranda's personality emerges, showing more welcoming and nuanced opinions of her employees. It ends on a good note, showing there are leaders frantically driving the business, while dealing politely and quietly with those who drive *them*.

THE PROPOSAL (Incompetent bosses; employee evaluation)
Original title: The Proposal
Director: Anne Fletcher
Cast: Sandra Bullock, Ryan Reynolds
Country: USA
Year: 2009

Sandra Bullock (Margaret) is a ruthless manager at a major office. Everyone is afraid of her. Each morning they prepare to make a good impression on her, and send each other emails announcing when the witch has arrived. However, as a Canadian immigrant, she must keep her Visa current in the United States, so she forces her assistant (Andrew) to marry her, a decision that polarizes the rest of the film.

The first part of the film deals with the manager concept in a very realistic way. Margaret is demanding and able to make tough decisions, but also has a keen eye for the people under her, and is not influenced by the excuses she hears, nor by her employee's outbursts.

WHAT WOMEN WANT (Incompetent bosses; Employee evaluation)
Original title: What Women Want
Director: Nancy Meyers
Cast: Mel Gibson, Helen Hunt
Country: USA
Year: 2000

Mel Gibson plays a hotshot chauvinistic executive at an advertising agency. When the company decides to focus on a female audience, his life is turned sideways, and a fluke accident enables him to hear what women think.

He discovers the world of female feelings, tastes, and perceptions—all new to him. He also makes the painful discovery of knowing what the women in his office think about him as a boss. He uses this to his advantage and becomes very successful in his advertising work; he also gets to woo Helen Hunt, his rival and boss until then.

The film shows real views on managers, bonding issues resulting from arrogance, and the need to refine the diagnosis of what's wrong with an employee to deal effectively with the situation.

CASUAL DAY (Various types of incompetent people)
Original title: Casual Day
Director: Max Lemcke
Cast: Juan Diego, Luis Tosar, Javier Ríos
Country: Spain
Year: 2007

Employees at a company in Madrid go to a country house to perform group integration activities. A business psychologist conducts the meetings, while maintaining private conversations with some of them. Various incompetent profiles begin to emerge: the timid person, the wimp, the jerk, the overwhelmed employee.

There is a strong contrast between sophisticated in-company training activities (musical instruments, paintball) and very confrontational personal and professional relationship concerns. Issues such as envy, blackmail, emotional rewards, management arrogance, manipulation, dismissal, and sexual harassment make the situation very tense.

The film takes delight in the managerial and HR functions in their most cruel versions, between group dynamics and pastoral landscapes. However, in its exaggeration, it manages to show the misery of many work environments. Not recommended for anyone who is thinking about organizing in-house management workshops.

GLENGARRY GLEN ROSS (Success at any cost; Types of incompetent people)
Original title: Glengarry Glen Ross
Director: James Foley
Cast: Al Pacino, Jack Lemmon, Alec Baldwin, Ed Harris, Alan Arkin, Kevin Spacey
Country: USA
Year: 1992

Based on a play by David Mamet, the film reflects on the hard life of salesmen, and by extension the new urban professionals of a major service firm. The star-studded cast injects an unusual power into this low-budget movie.

Times are tough at the branch, and a supervisor from the downtown office introduces a new incentive system: the top salesperson gets a Cadillac, the second a set of knives, and the third prize is you get to hit the bricks; one of the most memorable scolding speeches comes from Alec Baldwin.

All the characters are priceless. Some of the fast-talking dialogues are worth memorizing. The phone calls show some of the most scripted selling tactics. Each of the salesmen has a difference set of circumstances: style, family status, experience, self-esteem, and the place each occupies in his professional skills life cycle. This is one rare example of how fiction can delve into the depths of reality.

IN GOOD COMPANY (Firing; Influencing; Work-life balance)
Original title: In Good Company
Director: Paul Weitz
Cast: Dennis Quaid, Scarlett Johansson, Topher Grace
Country: USA
Year: 2004

Though a sentimental plot, plus someone like Scarlett Johansson, can somewhat blur the business-related aspect of the film, it has plenty of good scenes that address key issues of someone who manages people. After a corporate takeover, a 26 year-old man ends up as an ad sales manager for the *Sports America* magazine, at the head of a department with professionals who have more age and experience than him.

Although at first he seems to behave as an aggressive and ruthless executive, he slowly starts listening to his employees and thinks over his decisions. This movie addresses the issue of firing someone with realism, as well as the difficulty of earning the trust of staff and customers. There are many intense meetings and interviews and a lot of content. Employees are evaluated for dismissal or promotion. His top employee is twice his age, and the young executive ends up falling for his daughter.

HOUSE (TV Series) (Employee evaluation; Management style)
Original title: House
Creator: David Shore
Cast: Hugh Laurie
Country: USA
Year: 2004

Gregory House is a diagnostic genius who leads a team of gifted doctors at Princeton-Plainsboro University Hospital. He gets the most serious and rare cases. House is convinced, as demonstrated in each episode, that there is no sensible treatment if you don't know the pathology behind the symptoms. The cure could be worse than the disease.

He always ends up with the correct diagnosis after a dramatic race-against-the-clock and trial-and-error process of elimination, searching through different interpretations to make sense out of very confusing symptoms. In his analysis, he uses experimental methods, a blackboard, checks other case records, explores medical records, searches in the patient's home, questions the patient's entourage, and undertakes harsh clinical sessions where the debate is thick with relentless criticism.

At the other end of the scale, Dr. House is convinced of his absolute intellectual superiority; he shows extreme cynicism, plays with other people's emotions, and manipulates them. He tends to alienate everyone (patients, physicians, hospital management). A phrase defines his philosophy: "What would you prefer—a doctor who holds your hand while you die, or one who ignores you while you get better?" At the end of the second season, his entire team abandons him and he is forced to rebuild it.

OFFICE SPACE (Employee evaluation)
Original title: Office Space
Director: Mike Judge
Cast: Ron Livingston, Stephen Root, Gary Cole
Country: USA
Year: 1999

One of the most sophisticated parodies of the business environment. A consultant is hired to analyze the workers' problems. One of the characters is a jerk, has his own way, breaks the rules and schedules, and never gets the job done. His friend is the opposite: introverted, rigorous, and hardworking.

The report recommends firing the hard worker and promoting the jerk, raising his salary and giving him complete freedom. The film has an unexpected and apocalyptic end.

PULP FICTION (Manager's role; Giving instructions; Gratitude)
Original title: Pulp Fiction
Director: Quentin Tarantino
Cast: John Travolta, Samuel L. Jackson, Harvey Keitel, Uma Thurman
Country: USA
Year: 1994

The entire "Bonny Situation" scene is a parody of the functions of an executive. I have no idea where Tarantino got the inspiration, or what bad experience he had with a boss that led him to it. Harvey Keitel appears on the scene to clean up the mess of two incompetent hit men:

"I'm Winston Wolfe. I solve problems.... If my help's not appreciated, then lotsa luck, gentlemen."

Although at first it seems that the Wolf's attitude is a bit dictatorial and completely superfluous, a detailed analysis shows great people management skills. The Wolf earns his keep: He defines a process, keeps up the pace, gives precise instructions, checks what can go wrong, gets resources, assumes responsibilities, and performs a differential diagnosis of his people. Despite his rough style, he ends up winning his "subordinates" over to his side.

THE OFFICE (TV Series) (Incompetent managers; Diagnosing incompetence; Scolding, rewarding, and punishing)
Original title: The Office
Creator: Greg Daniels
Cast: Steve Carell, Rainn Wilson, John Krasinski
Country: USA
Year: 2005

One of the best series taking on the subject of life at a company. It's about a paper company, but the industry sector is not important. The lead character in the original English version, David Brent, is the head of an office with fewer than 20 employees. He has a high opinion of his management style and he's lighthearted, humorous, and thinks of himself as very approachable. He closely follows the development of his staff and organizes events and parties to enhance that good relationship he assumes he has.

But the opinion that the employees have of their boss is totally the opposite. They see him as tacky, trying too hard to be funny, stealing ideas and taking credit for them, and doing nothing to get the job done. He rates people on superficial criteria and is always starting petty squabbles.

The series lets you practice employee evaluations, and assess the use of many basic managerial tools: thanking, celebrating, correcting, rewarding, punishing, and so on.

RATATOUILLE (Each manager a teacher; Trade)
Original title: Ratatouille
Director: Brad Bird
Cast (voices): Patton Oswalt, Brian Dennehy, Brad Garrett
Country: USA
Year: 2007

In this animated film, Remy is a rat with a wonderful sense of smell and taste who has the potential to become a high-end chef. In the sewers of the city, the ghost of a famous and recently deceased chef, Gusteau, appears to Remy on the pages of the chef's book, *Anyone Can Cook*, and urges the rat to take that path.

The whole film is a hymn to craft, the taste for good food, and the love for work, training, and teamwork. Its basic message is that talent can be found in the most unexpected places, and that it is worthwhile to put it to use.

KARATE KID (Training; Setting the basics)
Original title: Karate Kid
Director: John G. Avildsen
Cast: Ralph Macchio, Noriyuki "Pat" Morita, Elisabeth Shue
Country: USA

No other classic movie better shows the need for training and learning to carry out an activity successfully (a fight, in this case). An elderly Japanese sensei prepares Daniel calmly and meticulously for an unparalleled fight. The pace of the film helps to convey the need for patience.

The lessons it contains are many and eloquent: The slope you must climb, the need for basic skills, toughness and repetition as a way of learning, and emotional aspects (willpower, self-control, resilience), are all required for success.

THE REMAINS OF THE DAY (Craft; Love for work)
Original title: The Remains of the Day
Director: James Ivory
Cast: Anthony Hopkins, Emma Thompson
Country: United Kingdom
Year: 1993

Despite criticism for Anthony Hopkins' emotional portrayal of butler Stevens, I consider his professional side exemplary. I am not sure whether reading Ishiguro's book before watching the movie had an impact, but I see the story as perfect praise for a job well done, seeing work as a service, the sense of craft, and how each person's small contribution fits together in the whole.

Stevens prepares things diligently, distributes tasks, calculate risks, and tries to correct what goes wrong. He takes time to sharpen his axe by reading; he knows customs and traditions. Besides, he practices the virtues of listening, giving and receiving advice, and obeying the master of the house.

LIFE IS BEAUTIFUL (Constructive vision; Teaching how to work)
Original title: La vita è bella
Director: Roberto Benigni
Cast: Roberto Benigni, Nicoletta Braschi
Country: Italy
Year: 1997

I am sure you will agree with me that this is one of the best movies ever. But I'm not sure if you know that it was inspired by Victor Frankl's motivational theories. This Jewish Viennese psychiatrist was imprisoned in a concentration camp and discovered how some people were able to keep their spirits up: by having a reason to live, a project to undertake, a destination, a meaning.

Life Is Beautiful is a very well-rounded film in many ways, a true work of art filled with details from which to learn. I especially like some scenes from the first part, when Guido arrives from the countryside to work as a waiter at his uncle's hotel. He teaches him unforgettable lessons on craft, technique, and love for work.

TWELVE O'CLOCK HIGH (Scolding and discipline)
Original title: Twelve O'Clock High
Director: Henry King
Cast: Gregory Peck, Hugh Marlowe, Dean Jagger
Country: USA
Year: 1949

This film is a gem of the management process. General Savage (Gregory Peck) takes over a southern England Air Command developed to bomb German cities, which is going through a gloom-laden period with little military effectiveness and morale hitting rock-bottom.

He is determined to restore discipline and order from the moment he arrives. And for this purpose, he makes wide use of correction. He wants to raise the bar for his troops, and though he's certain to fail, after a clever ploy he ends up earning everyone's respect.

GRAN TORINO (Gratitude and forgiveness)
Original title: Gran Torino
Director: Clint Eastwood
Cast: Clint Eastwood
Country: USA
Year: 2008

Walt Kowalski (Clint Eastwood) is a retired widower on a small pension and a veteran of the Korean War who lives alone in an area inhabited by different ethnic groups. This leads to altercations. Violent gangs are infesting the neighborhood. Walt's prize possessions are a rifle and a Ford Gran Torino. He can't get along with his children.

The house next door is occupied by a family of Hmong immigrants from Southeast Asia. Kowalski, against his will at first, saves his neighbors' child from a brawl. From here, a relationship develops, with expressions of gratitude that keep escalating. Eventually, the grumpy old man ends up acting like a hero, apologizes, and makes peace with himself.

GLADIATOR (Manager role; Forgiveness)
Original title: Gladiator
Director: Ridley Scott
Cast: Russell Crowe, Richard Harris
Country: USA and UK
Year: 2000

A colossal war takes place at the height of the Roman Empire. Shortly before his death, Emperor Marcus Aurelius chooses Maximus to be his heir over his own son, Commodus, due to concerns over emotional intelligence. But the conflict has only just begun.

With the struggles of Maximus (Russell Crowe), *Gladiator* elaborates the qualities needed to assume leadership leadership styles, and their impact on the degree of adhesion of the subjects, and the role of tactical and technical capabilities. Above all, it exposes the incredible qualities (in their most strict meaning) of a peaceful, humble, forgiving management model that is both trusting and trustworthy.

INVICTUS (Forgiveness and reconciliation)
Original title: Invictus (Playing the Enemy)
Director: Clint Eastwood
Cast: Morgan Freeman, Matt Damon
Country: USA
Year: 2009

This is a film adaptation of journalist John Carlin's book, *Playing the Enemy: Nelson Mandela and the Game That Changed a Nation.*

After the apartheid regime, the accumulated resentment against whites in South Africa's black population was at its highest point. With the country moving from marginalizing the black majority to marginalizing the white minority, it seemed impossible to integrate the two communities.

Nelson Mandela is elected president. And, surprising both sides, he begins a process of national reconciliation, taking advantage of the unifying social force of sports. Twenty-eight years of imprisonment and hard labor did not make Mandela descend into a spiral of revenge, but forged in him an attitude of inner peace and turned him into a peacemaker.

In the film, there are many examples of understanding, stepping into the shoes of the other person, compromising and negotiating, camaraderie and cooperation. But above all, Mandela shines by walking into the field, listening and personally meeting his collaborators, influencing with soft words, proposing ambitious and worthwhile challenges, and developing professional, emotional, and human talents in those around him. The most impressive fact is that everything in this film is true.

Acknowledgments

Apology Credits

I apologize to all those mentioned in the book if I misunderstood the meaning of their words. I have often been driven by the Italian idiom, "Se non è vero, è ben trovato," which could be translated: "Even if it's not true, it's a good story."

I apologize to those who accidentally took center stage in some half-invented unconstructive stories; I appreciate them, and they have contributed a lot to what I know about management.

I apologize to the many authors who have inspired me in form or substance but whom I failed to quote for some reason.

I apologize to my wife and seven children for snapping at them here and there while engaged in my writing, and for not spending quality time with them on my days off, due to this reason.

Thank-You Credits

Thanks to Javier Fernández Aguado for believing that someone in his 40 who had never written a book, could do so and do so well.

Thanks to Paco Lopez and Libros de Cabecera, who welcomed a book that the financial crisis had orphaned. And who also offered me valuable information to finish shaping it.

Thanks to Lluís Amiguet, clearly the second person contributing additional text to this book, who with his professionalism as a great interviewer stands out by not wanting to stand out. He and I gave seminars based on the stories from *La Contra* of *La Vanguardia*.

Thanks to Patricia Vázquez-Dodero who, when I mentioned I was looking for a book topic, made me see what I had before me.

Thanks to all the bosses I've had, those who have taught me important tidbits for good management, and especially those who have allowed me to refine the catalog of incompetence.

Thanks to all my friends, clients, and colleagues, some of them explicitly mentioned, who have shown that reality usually is stranger than fiction.

Thanks to Juan Ramirez and Jordi García Bon, my partners at Andersen, who bet on me at a crossroads that completed my profile as a business consultant, and also to my other colleagues, from whom I have copied a lot.

Thanks to the students of the Universitat Abat Oliba CEU, especially those who have studied people management in recent years; they have endured this book as subject matter, with greater willingness than I could have expected.

Thanks to all my students, who already number in the thousands, from whom I have verified that the number of incompetent people is infinite, in the positive and ironic meaning of this book.

Thanks to the many movies, some mentioned here, which, besides entertaining me, have given me graphic examples of good and bad management styles.

Thanks to those who have contributed to shaping the text: Elisabet in the appendix, and Adrian Portalo and Juan Lazaro in transcribing some of the texts. Thanks to Pepe, who has always believed that I had something to say, despite evidence to the contrary.

Thanks to the illustrious Collegi d'Advocats of Barcelona, where much of this work has been written.

Thanks to all those I failed to mention but who have contributed a lot or a little, wittingly or unwittingly, to the contents of this book:

authors, colleagues, teachers, and characters in the anecdotes, which were rarely invented.

Thanks to BarÇa coach Pep Guardiola, who has shown the entire world that the "better the devil you know than the devil you don't" strategy is not only very amusing, profoundly human, and profitable, but also one leading to success.

Thanks to IESE Professor Juan Antonio Pérez López, who now, in some corner of the universe, is creating solar systems, as he always wished to do; this is the result of our many hours of conversation and intellectual stimulation. He bet on me when I was in disarray from my college studies, and brought me to the current point in my business philosophy. And to Trini Santos, my background muse on many issues. And to Alejandro Llano, who always encouraged me with his permanent smile, always welcoming and smart.

Thanks to a group of 12 people who set the tone for the great project that is the Abat Oliba CEU University. Never before have I seen a group of professors (and I'm on my fourth university) with such intelligence, academic eminence, study skills, brilliance, honesty, and humbleness of soul.

Thanks to my small family (Bet, Imma, Oriol, Laia, Joan, Anna, Pol, and Maria, my wife), who have given me food for thought and encouragement to continue, and the means to be able to finish. Also to my larger family of brothers and cousins scattered through the world whom I have used for reference, whose prominent academic guidance has justified the presence of a shelf of books written by the family in my living room, where I haven't been until now.

And thanks to my parents who bet on me before knowing the potential talent I might have.

References

Adam, S. (1996). *The Dilbert Principle*. New York: HarperBusiness.

Amela, V. Interview with Moebius. *La Vanguardia*, July 4, 2011.

Amiguet, L. Interview with David Goleman. *La Vanguardia*, February 20, 1999.

Amiguet, L. Interview with El Juli. *La Vanguardia*, April 1999.

Amiguet, L. Interview with Richard Boyatzis. *La Vanguardia*, October 13, 2005.

Amiguet, L. Interview with Humberto Maturana. *La Vanguardia*, November 7, 2005.

Amiguet, L. Interview with José Ángel Carrey. *La Vanguardia*, February 16, 2008.

Amiguet, L. Interview with Ken Blanchard. *La Vanguardia*, May 25, 2008.

Aquinas, T. (c. 1265). *Summa Theologica*, Vol. II, Part II. (New York: Cosimo, 2013).

Aristotle. (n.d). *Nicomachean Ethics*, Book IV. (Indianapolis, IN: Hackett, 1999).

Bird, B., and J. Pinkava. *Ratatouille*. Emeryville, CA: Pixar, 2007.

Blake, R. and J. Mouton. (1964). *The Managerial Grid: The Key to Leadership Excellence*. Houston, TX: Gulf Publishing Co.

Chevrot, G. (2010). *Las Pequeñas Virtudes del Hogar*. Barcelona, Spain: Herder.

Cicero. (c. 44 B.C.). *De Officiis*, trans. Walter Miller (Cambridge, MA: Harvard University Press, 1913).

Covey, S. (1989). *The 7 Habits of Highly Effective People*. New York: Free Press.

El-Ghandouri, L. (2007). *El Despido Interior*. Barcelona, Spain: Alienta.

Fallon, I. (1989). *The Brothers: The Saatchi & Saatchi Story*. Chicago, IL: Contemporary Books.

Fayol, H. (1916). *Administration Industrielle et Générale; Prévoyance, Organisation, Commandement, Coordination, Controle*. Paris: H. Dunod et E. Pinat.

Fernández Aguado, J. (2007). *Dirigir Personas en la Empresa: Enfoque Conceptual y Aplicaciones Prácticas*. Madrid, Spain: Editorial Pirámide.

Fernandez, T. "Los Directivos Suspenden en Gestión." Expansión.com. Posted December 15, 2010. Accessed at http://www.expansion.com/2010/10/15/empleo/desarrollo-de-carrera/1287152586.html.

Ferrado, M. L. "Jefes Tóxicos." *El País*, January 12, 2008.

Ginebra, J. (1976). "La Maduracion de los Mercados y la Estrategia Comercial de los Negocios." Pamplona, Spain: Ediciones Universidad de Navarra.

Goula, J. "They Have Not Learned How to Lead." *La Vanguardia*, November 30, 2003.

Gracián, B. (1637). *The Art of Worldy Wisdom.* (Boston, MA: Shambala Publications, 2004).

Hersey, P. and K. H. Blanchard. (1977). *Management of Organizational Behavior: Utilizing Human Resources*, 3rd edition. New Jersey: Prentice Hall.

Hunter, J. (1998). *The Servant: A Simple Story About the True Essence of Leadership.* New York: Crown Business.

IESE. (2007). *IESE Alumni* magazine. Barcelona, Spain.

Luciani, A. (1978). *Illustrissimi: The Letters From Pope John Paul I.* Boston, MA: Little, Brown, and Company.

Otto Walter. (2007). "Cuáles Son las Conductas Más Desquiciantes de los Empleados Tóxicos?" Investigación Otto Walter 2007.

Pattakos, A. (2010). *Prisoners of Our Thoughts: Viktor Frankl's Principles for Discovering Meaning in Life and Work.* San Francisco, CA: Berrett-Koehler.

Roca i Junyent, M. (2007). *¡Sí, Abogado! Lo Que No Aprendí en la Facultad.* Barcelona, Spain: Crítica.

Royo Marín, A. (2007). *Teología Moral Para Seglares: I, Moral Fundamental y Especial.* Madrid, Spain: Biblioteca de Autores Cristianos.

Sahlins, M. (1968). *Tribesmen.* NJ: Prentice Hall.

Sanchís, I. Interview with Jorge Wagensberg. *La Vanguardia*, January 13, 2002.

Seneca. (n.d.). *On Anger.*

Sennet, R. (1998). *The Corrosion of Character: The Personal Consequences of Work in the New Capitalism.* New York: W.W. Norton & Company.

Tuckman, B. (1965). *Developmental Sequence in Small Groups.* Psychological Bulletin 63(6): 384–99.

Wagensberg, J. (2006). *A Más Cómo, Menos por Qué: 747 Reflexiones con la Intención De Comprender lo Fundamental, lo Natural y lo Cultural.* Barcelona, Spain: Tusquets Editores.

About the Author

Gabriel Ginebra began his career as a professor at the Institute of Higher Business Studies (IESE) School of Business at the University of Navarra, and later taught at academic institutions throughout Spain. He has an MBA and a doctoral degree in workplace organization. He has directed consulting projects for companies in a wide range of industries, including finance, pharmacy, healthcare, logistics, and media. Currently Gabriel is a professor of management skills at the University Abat Oliba CEU of Barcelona. He directed the Nicomachean project, which combines classical thought with management competencies. Gabriel's blog can be viewed at http://gestiondeincompetentes.com/.